BIBLE WARNINGS

BIBLE WARNINGS

SERMONS FOR CHILDREN
ON DANGERS ALONG THE PATH
AND HOW TO AVOID THEM

RICHARD NEWTON

Author of *Heroes of the Early Church, Heroes of the Reformation, Bible Promises, The Safe Compass, Rays from the Sun of Righteousness, The Life of Jesus Christ for the Young,* and *The King's Highway*

Solid Ground Christian Books
Birmingham, Alabama USA

Solid Ground Christian Books
715 Oak Grove Road
Birmingham, AL 35209
205-443-0311
sgcb@charter.net
http://solid-ground-books.com

BIBLE WARNINGS
Sermons for Children on Dangers along the Path
And How to Avoid Them

Richard Newton (1813-1887)

Taken from 1886 edition by Robert Carter & Brothers, NY

Solid Ground Classic Reprints

First printing of new edition June 2006

Cover work by Borgo Design, Tuscaloosa, AL
Contact them at nelbrown@comcast.com

Special thanks to Ric Ergenbright for permitting us to use the beautiful photograph on the cover. Please visit his new and expanded web site at ricergenbright.com

ISBN: 1-89925-083-7

PREFACE.

In travelling along our great railroads, at all the principal stopping-places we find signal stations. In connection with each of these, there is a man appointed, one of whose duties is to watch that the road is kept in order. If a bridge should be broken, or any unusual obstruction should be found on that road, he is expected to ring a bell, or wave a flag, or make a signal of some kind, so that the conductor of any train, coming along the road, may know about the difficulty, in time to stop his train before any harm is done. And the bell which that station man rings, or the flag which he waves, or the signal which he puts out, is the *warning* given to approaching trains to save them from injury.

In the journey that we are pursuing, through this mortal life, we are sure to meet with many dangers. The Bible, is the guide-book, which God has given us to use on this journey. And the warnings found in this Book, are the bells, which God has caused to be rung, or the flags to be waved, or the signals to be put out, to tell us of the dangers that lie along our path, in order that we may avoid them. We cannot be safe in our journey through the world, unless we are careful to mind these warnings. This course of sermons has been written, and this volume containing them has been published, with the hope of helping the young to understand these warnings, and so escape the dangers to which they refer.

That it may please God to bless the book, and make it useful in this way, is the earnest prayer of the writer.

R. N.

CONTENTS.

I.	THE WARNING NOT TO FORGET GOD .	9
II.	THE WARNING AGAINST COVETOUSNESS .	34
III.	THE WARNING AGAINST INTEMPERANCE	60
IV.	THE WARNING AGAINST THE TRANSGRESSOR'S WAYS.	91
V.	THE WARNING AGAINST LYING . . .	114
VI.	THE WARNING AGAINST SIN. . . .	138
VII.	THE WARNING AGAINST ANGER. . .	162
VIII.	THE WARNING AGAINST GRIEVING THE SPIRIT	186
IX.	THE WARNING AGAINST BREAKING THE SABBATH	214
X.	THE WARNING AGAINST PRIDE . . .	239
XI.	THE WARNING AGAINST SLOTHFULNESS	261
XII.	THE WARNING AGAINST DISCONTENT .	285
XIII.	THE WARNING AGAINST DISOBEYING OUR PARENTS	309
XIV.	THE WARNING AGAINST SWEARING . .	334
XV.	THE WARNING AGAINST SELFISHNESS .	356

I.

THE WARNING NOT TO FORGET GOD.

"Remember now thy Creator in the days of thy youth."
ECCLESIASTES xii. 1.

WE enter now on a new course of sermons for the young. Our last course we called "Bible Promises." The present one we may call "*Bible Warnings.*" It is very important that we should know about the warnings which are given us in the Bible, and that we should mind them too.

Suppose that you and I owned a nice pleasure steam yacht, and that during one of our summer holidays, we should undertake to sail all round the coast of England, or along our own Atlantic coast, from Maine to Texas. As we went on with our voyage, we should find at every little distance a light-house, lifting itself up towards the sky. And when night came on and it was dark, we should see that the lamp was kindled at the top of each light-house, and was kept burning all night. Now what are those lighthouses for? Why in each place where one of them stands, there is a dangerous rock or shoal, and the light-houses are built and the lamps in them are kept burning, to let the sailors know just where those dangers are, in order that they may keep clear of them. Light-houses are like warnings. When the sailor sees them he knows that there are rocks or shoals near them. To sail on them would wreck or ruin his ship, and so he steers clear of them, and in doing this he finds safety. And the warnings of the Bible are like light-houses which God has put in dangerous places for our safety. And I pray that God may make this course of sermons useful to all who hear or read them, by enabling us to keep out of the way of the dangers to which these " Bible Warnings " refer.

Our first text in this course is—" Remember now thy Creator in the days of thy youth." Some may say that this is a command, rather than a warning. That is so. But it may be taken either as a command, or a warning. It is a command to remember God ; or it is a warning not to forget God, when we are young. And so

THE WARNING NOT TO FORGET GOD. 11

we may say that the subject of our present sermon is—*the warning not to forget God when we are young.*

And there are three reasons why we should mind this warning, and not forget God when we are young.

In the first place we ought to mind this warning for THE LORD'S SAKE.

Our first illustration may be called—

MINDING GOD.

"I wish I could mind God, as my little dog minds me," said a little boy, looking thoughtfully at his shaggy friend—"he always seems so pleased to mind, and I don't."

That little dog obeyed his young master, for his master's sake. He really loved him, and tried to show this love by the cheerful, ready way in which he obeyed him. This was the right thing for him to do ; and it is just what God expects us to do. When He says—"Remember now thy Creator in the days of thy youth," He means that we should do this for His sake, to show our love to Him; just as that little dog showed his love to his master, by doing gladly, and cheerfully, whatsoever he told him to do.

Our next illustration may be called—

THE ONE GIFT.

There is one gift which we may all make to God, and which He will value more than anything else we can possibly offer to Him. It is that to which He refers when He says—"My son, give me thine heart." If we had millions of money, and we should offer it all to God, it would be worth nothing to Him, unless we first gave Him our hearts.

A little Sabbath-school girl brought a present to her teacher of a bouquet of beautiful flowers.

"And why do you bring me these?" asked her teacher.

"Because I love you," was her quick reply.

"And do you bring anything to Jesus?" asked the teacher.

"O yes," was her reply—"I have given my heart to Jesus." That was a beautiful answer. And that is just what Jesus expects each one of us to do. He wants us to remember Him in our youth, and to give Him our hearts, as this little girl had done. And He wants us to do this for His own sake, and out of love to Him. And then everything we do for Him, and everything we give to Him, will be pleasing, and acceptable to Him.

There is one more illustration about a little boy, who said—

"I WANT TO DO SOMETHING FOR GOD."

He was a pale, sickly-looking little fellow, and was seated in the kitchen of a small cottage, and was occupied in reading his Bible. His mother was sitting by, busily engaged in sewing, when she was suddenly surprised to hear him exclaim —"O mother, I'm so happy!" The little fellow rose from his seat, and coming towards her he laid his head on her lap.

The mother's eyes filled with tears, for she knew that her little boy had very few things to make him happy. He was sick and lame, and they were so poor that he had neither warm clothes, nor proper food ; but she only said— " Well, my dear boy, and what is it that makes you so happy?" The boy lifted up his pale thin face, and said : "O mother dear, it's because I do so love God ; and He is so good."

"And pray what has put this into your mind, just now?" asked his mother.

"Why, I've been reading in the Bible about His goodness in many things; and above all His greatest goodness in sending Jesus into our world to die for us. O mother, when I think of all that God has done, and Jesus has suffered for us, I cannot help wishing that I could do something for God."

"But what can you do, my child?" said his mother. "You are too weak and sick to work."

"I know that, mother; but I *must* do something. I believe that I shall not live very long, and I want to try and show that I would do good if I could. Won't you get me a Missionary box and let me try to fill it?"

"I am quite willing, my dear boy, to do that; only you must not be asking all the ladies who come here to see you, for money: that you know would not be pleasant."

"No, mother, I won't do that; but I've been thinking that I might sell the little wooden knives and toothpicks, which I make, and cut out more of the paper ornaments, that Mrs. Williams liked so much. Perhaps the ladies will buy them."

" Well, my boy, I'll get the paper, and when father comes home you can ask him for some wood."

In a week from that time that dear boy, whose name was Jimmie, had several little articles neatly finished, and laid on a paper tray, upon which was a card, with these words written on it—" For sale, for the benefit of the Missionary Society."

In a very short time, the kind ladies who came to see him, and bring work for his mother, bought all the things which were on the tray, for they felt pleased to encourage the little fellow who was so earnest to do good ; and Jimmie soon found that his efforts to "do something for God," were blessed by Him, and made successful.

When the next quarterly Missionary meeting was held, in the church which they attended, Jimmie's mother carried his Missionary-box and gave it into the minister's hands, saying—" It's my son Jimmie's box, sir "—and then she burst into tears, for her dear boy was dead. He had been seized with a sudden illness, in the midst of his efforts for the Missionary cause, and after lingering a week had died.

The box was opened, and found to contain eighteen shillings and sixpence, or nearly five dollars of our money. And this sum was soon increased by the sale of all the other articles which Jimmie had left on his paper tray.

Jimmie had minded the warning given in our text, against forgetting God. He remembered his Creator in the days of his youth. And his desire to "do something for God," showed that he was doing it for the Lord's sake. The first reason why we should mind the warning of our text, is for the Lord's sake.

The second reason why we should do this, is— FOR OUR OWN SAKE.

When we really begin to remember God, and to keep His commandments, God says to each of us, as he said to the Israelites in old times—"from this day will I bless you." And God's blessing is worth more to us than all the world beside. If the wealth of all the rich men in the world were ours, it would do us no good without God's blessing. But that blessing can make us happy, without any of the gold and silver which men prize so much. When the good poet Cowper was speaking on this point, he looked up to his God and Saviour and said:

"Give what Thou wilt, without Thee we are poor,
But with Thee rich, take what Thou wilt away."

And this is true. If we only have God with us, He can supply the place of all other things; but there is nothing else that can supply His place. And so we see how important it is *for our own sakes* that we should "remember our Creator in the days of our youth." Our peace, our safety, our usefulness, our happiness, our everything, depends upon it.

Now let us look at some illustrations of this part of our subject. The first incident shows us the evil that must follow, if we do not remember our Creator, when he calls upon us to do so. We may call it—

NOT YET.

"Remember now thy Creator" was once said to a little boy.

"Not yet," said the boy, as he busied himself

with his bat and ball; "when I grow older I will think about it."

The little boy grew to be a young man.

"Remember *now* thy Creator," his conscience said to him.

"Not yet," said the young man; "I am now about to begin my trade; when I see my business prosper, I shall have more time than I can command now."

His business did prosper.

"Remember *now* thy Creator," conscience whispered to him.

"Not yet," said the man of business; "my children must now have my care; when they are settled in life, I shall be better able to attend to the claims of religion."

He lived to be a gray-headed old man.

"Remember *now* thy Creator," was the voice which conscience once more addressed to him.

"Not yet," was still his cry; "I shall soon retire from business, and then I shall have nothing else to do but read and pray."

Soon after this he died, without becoming a Christian. He put off to another time, what he should have attended to when young, and *that*

THE WARNING NOT TO FORGET GOD. 19

caused the loss of his soul. Those two little words—"*Not yet*"—were his ruin.

Our next story may be called—

JESSIE'S SIX CENTS.

Some time ago a pale-faced little girl walked hastily into a book store in Boston, and said to the man who was serving at the counter—

"Please, sir, I want a book that's got 'Suffer little children to come unto me,' in it, and how much is it, sir? and I am in a great hurry."

The shopkeeper looked kindly at her for a moment, and said, "Well, suppose I haven't got the book you want, what then, my dear?"

"O, sir, I shall be very sorry; "I want it so much," and her little voice trembled at the thought of a disappointment.

The kind shopkeeper took her little hand in his, and said—"Will you be so very sad without the book, and why are you in such a hurry?"

"Well, sir, you see, I went to Sunday-school one Sunday, when Mrs. West, who takes care of me, was away; and the teacher read about a Good Shepherd, who spoke those words; and I want to go where He is. I'm so tired of being where there's nobody to care for a little girl like me, only Mrs. West, who is always saying I'd better be dead than alive."

"But why are you in such a hurry?" asked the bookseller.

"Why, you see, sir, my cough is getting bad, and I want to know all about this 'Good Shepherd' before I die; it would be so strange to see Him in heaven and not know Him. Besides sir, if Mrs. West knew I was here she'd take away the six cents I've saved by running errands, to buy the book, so I'm in a hurry to get served."

This touched the bookseller's heart very much, and filled his eyes with tears. Then he took off his spectacles and wiped them; and lifting a book down from the shelf, he said—"I'll find the words you want, my dear child; come and listen while I read them." Then he turned to the 15th verse of the 18th chapter of St. Luke, and read these words—"But Jesus called them"—*i. e.* the infants—"unto Him, and said, 'Suffer little children to come unto me, and forbid them not; for of such is the kingdom of God.' Then the good man told how this blessed Saviour has prepared a glorious home in heaven—a home of rest, and peace, and joy, and happiness, and where He will take all who love and serve Him, to live with Him forever.

"Oh! how lovely that is!" exclaimed the dear child in her eagerness. "He says 'Come.' I'll go to Him.—How long do you think it will be, sir, before I shall see Him?"

"Not long, perhaps," said the bookseller, turning aside his head, and wiping away the tears. "You may keep your six cents, and come here every day, and I will read to you some more about this good Friend and Saviour of little children."

Then she thanked him very heartily and hurried away. The next day came, and another, and another, but that little girl never returned to hear about Jesus.

One day, about two weeks after this, a coarse-looking woman, with a loud voice, ran into the book-store, saying—"Jessie's dead! She died talking about the good Shepherd, and she said you was to have these six cents for the Mission box at school. And as I don't like to keep dead people's money, here it is." And throwing the money down on the counter, she ran out of the shop.

The six cents went into the Missionary box, and when the story of Jessie was told, so many people followed her example in making offerings to the good cause, that by the end of the year, "Jessie's cents," as they were called, were found sufficient to send out a Missionary to China, to help in bringing lost sheep to the Good Shepherd.

Here we see how Jessie remembered her Creator, as soon as she heard of Him. And it was for *her own sake* she did it. She had no friend, no help, no comfort in the world, but she found everything she needed in Jesus. She never said—"Not yet," like the last person spoken of. But as soon as she heard of Jesus, she said " *Now* "—and came to Him at once. And this has made her happy forever.

I have one other illustration for this part of our subject. We may call it—

A CHILD'S FAITH.

In a town in Holland there once lived a very poor widow. One night her hungry children

THE WARNING NOT TO FORGET GOD.

asked her for some bread. With the tears streaming down her cheeks she said—"My darling children, how gladly I would do this if I could, but there is not a morsel of bread in the house." This poor woman was a Christian, and was trying to love and serve God.

She knew how good He is, and how He has promised to help His people when they are in trouble. So she gathered the children round her, and read a part of the fifth Psalm, ending with the fifteenth verse, in which is found the sweet promise, "Call on me in the day of trouble, and I will deliver thee." Then she prayed with them, telling the Lord of their trouble, and earnestly asking Him to help and deliver them.

On rising from their knees, her eldest child, a little boy about eight years old, said to her, "Mother, dear, are we not told in the Bible about one of God's prophets, who had food brought to him by the ravens?"

"Yes, my son, but that was a very long time ago," said his mother.

"But mother, what God has done once, can He not do again? Now I will go and open the door, that the birds may come in, and bring us some food."

Then the dear little fellow went and set the front door wide open, so that the light of their lamp shone out upon the sidewalk.

Now it happened just then, that the burgomaster of the town was going by. He was a kind-hearted Christian man. Seeing the door open, and the light shining out from the room, he thought it very strange, and stopped a moment. Then he entered the house, and asked, "why they left their door open on such a cold night as that?"

"My little boy did it, sir," said the mother, "that the ravens might come in, and bring some bread for the hungry children, for we have nothing to eat."

"Indeed," said the burgomaster; "then here is the raven already. Come with me, my boy, and you will soon see where the bread is to come from."

So he quickly led the boy to his own house, and sent him home with a basket full of bread, and butter, and meat, and potatoes, and lots of nice things. What a happy supper they had there that night! And after supper the little boy opened the front door again, and looking up to heaven, he said — "Many thanks, dear Father in heaven, for all the good things Thou hast sent us."

Now we can all see how truly it was for his own good, that *that* little boy had remembered his Creator in the days of his youth. The second reason why we ought to do this is—for our own sakes.

And then there is a third reason why we should mind the warning of the text, or—" remember our Creator in the days of our youth," and that is—

FOR THE SAKE OF OTHERS.

God's promise to Abraham, when he began to serve Him, was that he should *be a blessing*. And God says the same thing to all His people. When Jesus was on earth we are told that "He went about doing good." And he desires that all who love and serve him, should follow his example in this respect, and "tread in the blessed steps of His most holy life." And in doing this, we can make ourselves real blessings to those who are about us. We can help to lead them to Jesus, if they do not know Him already. And if they do know Him, we can speak words of comfort and encouragement to them. And not only by our words, but by our actions, and by our prayers, we may be doing good, all the time, to those about us.

When Joseph lived in the house of Potiphar, in Egypt, God blessed all that household for his sake. And when David, the king of Israel, came back from one of his warlike expeditions, we read that "he returned to bless his household." And this will be the case with us, if we "remember our Creator in the days of our youth," and become real earnest Christians. Then we shall be blessings wherever we go. Let us look now at some illustrations of the way in which this may be done. The first of these may be called—

GRANDPA'S STAR.

Grandpa was sick, and little Fannie loved to be with him, and to read to him. She would sit down by his bedside and say—"Shall I read my story, grandpa?"

And the story to which she referred was that

in the New Testament, which begins with "Now when Jesus was born in Bethlehem, there came wise men from the east to Jerusalem." She called it "my story," because she liked it so much, and she never got tired of reading it. One day, when she had finished reading, she said,

"Grandpa, you are a wise man, but you didn't have to take a long journey to find Jesus, like the wise men I was reading about, did you?"

"What makes you think I didn't?" asked grandpa, with a trembling voice.

"Because, grandpa, Jesus stays right by us, all the time; so we've only got to whisper to Him, and He hears us."

The days went on, and one evening, not long after this, all the family gathered round grandpa's bed to say "good-bye" to him before he died.

When he came to speak to little Fannie, he laid his hand gently on her head and said, "Good-bye, my darling. When I get to heaven, the beautiful city, I will tell the blessed Saviour that you were my star."

"O grandpa, why?" asked Fannie, as the tears streamed down her cheeks.

"Because, darling, you led me to Jesus, just as the star you have often read about, led the wise men to Him. And your light shone so steadily that I could not lose my way." And here we see how remembering her Creator in the days of her youth, made little Fannie a blessing to her grandpa. Our next illustration we may call—

RAINBOW REAGAN.

One day poor widow Reagan, who was a washerwoman, was hard at work over her tubs. As she rubbed away at the clothes, she got thinking about her many troubles, till one after another the tears were falling into the soap suds; but still she kept on with her work. Nobody was near to see her sorrow, but her little boy Jack, about five years old, who was playing with his blocks on the floor. He looked at his mother a moment, surprised to see her weeping, and then, under the influence of his love and pity, he pushed a chair up to the washbench, and climbing up on it, put his rosy, laughing face close by his mother's sad one, and throwing his arms round her neck kissed her

THE WARNING NOT TO FORGET GOD. 29

kindly. It made a pretty picture. Just then, Mrs. Reagan's minister happened to enter the cottage. He paused a moment, and gazed on the interesting sight before him. Then he said, "Now, Mrs. Reagan, you have rain and sunshine both together in this room. The bow of promise must be very near."

At this little Jack laughed aloud, and his mother smiled through her tears, and while she handed the minister a chair, she said—"Shure and yer riverence niver spake a truer word nor that same. My Jack is a rainbow that the Lord Himself has given me. And when I look into my darlint's face, and see his swate smile, I know, by that same token, that the Lord will not let my troubles overwhelm me."

I suppose the good minister probably told the story of the widow's tears, and her boy's smiles, for after that, Jack was always spoken of in the village by the name of, "Rainbow Reagan," and he proved by his conduct to his mother, that he well deserved that name.

Here we see what a blessing Jack was, by making sunshine in that home, which would otherwise have been made gloomy, and sad, by the tears of sorrow. He "remembered his Creator in the days of his youth," for the sake of others.

I have just one other illustration of this part of our subject. We may call it—

SAYING PLEASE.

It is about a little boy whose name was Bonnell. He was a very bright little fellow, about eight years old. His father was not a Christian, and they never had a blessing asked at their meals.

"Pa," said the little fellow, one day, "Ma says that God made you. Did he, pa?"

"Yes, he made me."

"Well, pa, are you glad he made you?"

"Why Bonnell, of course I am; what strange questions you do ask!"

The little fellow was evidently thinking about something which he could not exactly make out.

Not long after this, he went on a visit to his Uncle Sam's. This uncle was an earnest Christian. He always asked a blessing at their meals, and had family prayers, and the reading of the

THE WARNING NOT TO FORGET GOD. 31

scriptures every day. This led Bonnell to think very seriously about these things, and to wonder why his father didn't do as his uncle did.

The first time they were all sitting round the table at breakfast, after his return home, he asked—"Pa, what does Uncle Sam ask a blessing at table for?"

"I reckon it's because he wants to."

"He says he wants to thank God for his dinner, but I told him you worked for your dinner, and made it. God does not give it to you, does he, pa?"

"Well, yes; I suppose he gives me mine too."

Bonnell looked in astonishment, and then he went vigorously to work with his knife and fork. Presently he looked up again and asked—"Pa, does God want Uncle Sam to thank him?"

"Yes, child; I suppose he does."

Then the little fellow was silent again.

After awhile he said—"Pa, I'm mighty glad that God is not like you, for if He was we should never get anything more to eat, and then we'd starve."

"Why, Bonnell, what do you mean?"

"I was just thinking that you would not let sister have that apple the other day because she wouldn't say—'please;'—and if God was that sort of way, he never would give us anything more, because we don't thank him, as Uncle Sam does, and say please."

"Be quiet, Bonnell; you don't know what you are talking about." Bonnell was quiet. The rest of that meal was eaten in silence. Bonnell's father went to his office, to attend to the business of the day. But he could not forget what his little boy had said. It led him to see that he was not doing right, in acting as he did, in not thanking God for His many mercies. And to the surprise of his family, when they sat down to tea that night, the father said 'please.' He thanked God for their food, and asked His blessing upon it. And the change did not end there. Bonnell's father never rested till he became a Christian, and joined the church. And here we see what a blessing that little boy's desire to remember his Creator brought upon that family.

Now, where is our text to-day? Ecclesiastes xii. 1. What are the words of the text?

"Remember now thy Creator in the days of thy youth."

And what is the sermon about? The warning not to forget God, when we are young.

How many reasons did we have for minding this warning? Three.

In the first place, we ought to mind this warning, for whose sake? *For the Lord's sake.*

In the second place, we ought to mind it for whose sake? *For our own sake.*

And in the third place, we ought to mind it for whose sake? *For the sake of others.*

We cannot do this of ourselves; but if we pray to God for the help of His grace, then we shall be able to remember, and love, and serve Him all our days.

II.

THE WARNING AGAINST COVETOUSNESS.

" Take heed and beware of covetousness."—LUKE xii. 15.

THIS is a very important warning. Covetousness means the love of money. St. Paul tells us that "the love of money is the root of all evil." If you and I could go through all the families of this city, and find out all the wrong things that have been done under the influence of covetousness, or the love of money, how surprising it would be! If we should write these cases all down, they would make a very long catalogue. And that catalogue would embrace sins, or wrong doings of every possible kind. We should find that covetousness, or the love of money, had led men to lie, and cheat, and swear, and steal, and murder, and to commit all manner of sins.

Covetousness is like a dangerous rock in the sea of life, over which we have to sail. Multitudes of wrecks are scattered all around it. The warning of our text is like a light-house, which God has caused to be built upon this rock, to give us notice of the danger to be found here, in order that we may avoid it.

Our subject to-day is—*the warning against covetousness.* We ought to mind this warning for three reasons. And these reasons all refer to the injury that covetousness will do to us, if we give way to it.

The first reason why we should mind this warning is—THAT COVETOUSNESS WILL DESTROY OUR HAPPINESS.

The true secret of being happy is to mind what God tells us. This is what David means when he says: "Then shall I not be ashamed" —or then shall I be truly happy—"when I have respect unto all thy commandments." Psalm cxix. 6. This proves the truth of what has just been said—that minding God is the secret of true happiness. You remember it was just so with Adam and Eve, when they were in the garden of Eden. So long as they minded what God told them, they were perfectly happy. But as soon as they quit minding God, and made up their minds to eat of the fruit of the tree, of which God had said they must not eat, then they lost all their happiness.

And it is just the same with ourselves. God requires us to love Him with all our hearts, and to keep His commandments. If we do this, it will surely make us happy. But if we let the love of money, or any other feeling which God has forbidden, take the place of His love in our hearts, then it is impossible for us to be happy.

We have a very good illustration of this part of our subject in the Old Testament.

You remember that the prophet Elisha had a servant that waited upon him. His name was Gehazi. He was very happy in the service of his master, till he gave way to covetousness, or the love of money. This led him to commit a great sin, and that destroyed his happiness.

After Elisha had cured Naaman the Syrian of his leprosy, the healed man felt so grateful for the wonderful favor, that he wanted to make the prophet a valuable present, as a token of his thankfulness. But Elisha declined to receive anything from him. And after Naaman was gone, Gehazi's covetousness, or love of money, led him to say—"My master has refused to re-

THE WARNING AGAINST COVETOUSNESS. 37

ceive a present from Naaman, but I will go after him, and take something from him."

So he went, and overtook him. Then he told a lie. He said his master had sent him to ask for some money, and some clothing. Naaman made him a splendid present. It was more than one man could carry. So he sent two of his servants to carry the present for Gehazi. As soon as he got back, he stowed the present safely away, and then he went in, and stood before his master, as usual. Elisha asked him where he had been. Then he told another lie, and said he had not been anywhere. In a moment, to his surprise, Elisha told him all that he had been doing, and ended with these terrible words— "The leprosy therefore of Naaman, shall cleave unto thee, and to thy children forever!" And in a moment it came to pass, and Gehazi went out from his master's presence, never to return to it again; and "he went out a leper, as white as snow!" Thus Gehazi's covetousness lost him his situation, and destroyed his happiness for all the rest of his life.

Now let us look at some other illustrations of

the evils of covetousness. The first of these may be called—

THE MISER'S MISERY

There was once a nobleman living in Scotland who was very rich. But his covetousness, or love of money, was very great. Whenever he received any money, he turned it into gold and silver, and stowed it away in a great chest which he kept in a strong vault, that had been built for this purpose down in the cellar.

One day a farmer, who was one of his tenants, came in to pay his rent. But when he had counted out the money, he found that it was just one farthing short; yet this rich lord was such a miser that he refused the farmer a receipt for the money, until the other farthing was paid. His home was five miles distant. He went there, and came back with the farthing. He settled his bill, and got his receipt.

Then he said, " My lord, I'll give you a shilling, if you'll let me go down into your vault, and look at your money."

His lordship consented, thinking that was an easy way to make a shilling. So he led the farmer down into the cellar and opened his big chest, and showed him the great piles of gold and silver that were there. The farmer gazed at them for awhile, and then said :

"Now, my lord, I am as well off as you are."

"How can that be ?" asked his lordship.

"Why, sir," said the farmer, "you never use any of this money. All that you do with it, is to look at it. I have looked at it too, and so I'm just as rich as you are."

That was true. The love of that selfish lord for his money, made him think of it day and night, and the fear lest some robber should steal it, took away all his comfort and happiness, and made him perfectly miserable.

Our next story may be called—

A MAN MADE UNHAPPY BY HIS COVETOUSNESS.

A man called on a clergyman one day to converse with him. "Sir," said he, "I have been a professor of religion for several years, and yet I have never enjoyed that peace and happiness which I know a Christian ought to have."

"Well then," said the minister, " there must be some good cause for this. Doesn't your conscience accuse you of some secret sin that you have committed?"

"That is true," said the man. "Some years ago, when I was a clerk in the store of Mr. B., one of the first merchants in this city, a bundle of notes, amounting to $500, had been left out of the fireproof. I had to stay behind, after the store was closed that evening, to finish some writing. Just before leaving the office, I saw the bundle of notes. My love of money overcame my sense of right. I took that money, and I have never had a moment of peace or happiness since."

"Well, my friend," said the minister—"the thing for you to do is to return that money."

"I would gladly do that," said the man, "if it were possible. But I have no money, and cannot do it. O, sir, if you would be willing to see Mr. B., to tell him the story of my wrong doing in this matter, without telling him my name; let him know how sadly I feel about it; ask his forgiveness, and assure him that the money shall be returned, as soon as it can possibly be done, then I shall feel happy again." The minister did this. Mr. B. freely forgave the wrong which had been done to him. This relieved that man of his trouble, and the happiness which had been so long destroyed by his love of money was restored.

There is one other story under this part of our sermon. It may be called—

THE TERRIBLE EVIL OF COVETOUSNESS.

Three men, who were once travelling together, found a large sum of money on the road. To avoid being seen, they went into the woods near by, to count out the money, and divide it among themselves. They were not far from a village, and as they had eaten up all their food, they concluded to send one of their number, the youngest of the company, into the village to buy some more food, while they would wait there till he came back.

He started on his journey. While walking to the village, he talked to himself in this way: —" How rich my share of this money has made me! But how much richer I should be if I only had it all! And why can't I have it? It is easy enough to get rid of those other two men. I can get some poison in the village, and put it into their food. On my return I can say that I had my dinner in the village, and don't want to eat any more. Then they will eat the food, and die, and so I shall have all this money instead of only having one-third of it."

But while he was talking to himself in this way, his two companions were making a different arrangement. They said to each other—" It is not necessary that this young man should be connected with us. If he was out of the way, we could each have the half of this money instead of only a third. Let us kill him as soon as he comes back." So they got their daggers ready, and as soon as the young man came back they plunged their daggers into him and killed him.

They then buried his dead body, and sat down to eat their dinner of the poisoned food which had been brought to them. They had hardly finished their dinner before they were both seized with dreadful pains, which soon ended in their death. And here we see how the happiness, and the lives of those three men were destroyed by the love of money. The first reason why we ought to mind this warning, and beware of covetousness, is because it will destroy our happiness.

The second reason why we should mind this warning is—THAT COVETOUSNESS WILL INJURE OUR USEFULNESS.

One of the ways in which we can make ourselves useful is by the right use of our money. It is not necessary that we should be rich in order to be useful. If we are not covetous, we may do much good with very small sums of money. Here is an illustration of this. We may call it—

THE GOOD ONE PENNY DID.

There was a little boy, about seven years old, whose name was Willie. His sister was making up a box to send to a Missionary in India. She asked Willie one day, if he wouldn't like to put some things in her box. He had just begun to save up enough money to buy himself a new top. He only had one penny, and he told his sister he could not spare that. But after thinking over it for awhile he said to himself—"Well, I guess the heathen need the gospel more than I need a top. I'll let my penny go

44 BIBLE WARNINGS.

into sister's box." Then he offered her the penny. But she said she was not going to send money in the box, and that he had better buy something with his penny and then it could be put in the box. "What shall I buy?" he asked. "Why, suppose you buy a tract," said his sister.

Before going out to do this, Willie went up to his own room. Then he laid the penny on the bed, and kneeling down he offered a short prayer over it. He told the Lord that this was all the money he had ; and that he was going to buy a tract with it and send it out to India, in his sister's missionary box. He asked God to bless that tract, and make it the means of doing good to some soul in India. Then he went and bought the tract, and gave it to his sister to put in her box, and told her how he had prayed to God for His blessing to rest upon it. There was a blank leaf on the back of the tract. On that leaf his sister wrote this little history of the tract, and then put it in her box.

When that box arrived in India, the missionary, to whom it was sent, was engaged in learning the language of a distant tribe, among whose people he was anxious to have the gospel

THE WARNING AGAINST COVETOUSNESS. 45

introduced. One of the chiefs of that tribe was helping him to learn their language. When that chief was about to leave him and return home, the missionary gave him some of the things which had been sent him in that box. Among the rest he gave him little Willie's tract. That chief could read English very well. On his way home he read that tract. The little incident, written on the back of it, touched him much. It led him to read the New Testament, which the missionary had given him. This brought him to Jesus, and he became a Christian. Then he never rested till he got a missionary to come and live among his people, and preach the gospel to them. Before long a chapel was built in that village, and numbers of the natives attended its services, and became Christians. They were very earnest followers of Jesus, and used to go into the neighboring villages, and tell the people there what they had learned about the gospel. God's blessing rested on those efforts, and the result was, that within four or five years, from the time that Willie's tract was given to that chief, several hundred heathens were brought to Jesus, through the influence which it exerted. Now if Willie's love of money had kept him from giving that penny, we see how it would have injured his usefulness.

Let us look now at some other incidents which show how covetousness, or the love of money, injures the usefulness of those who give way to it. We have two good illustrations of this point in the Bible. One of these we find in Judas Iscariot. He was one of the twelve men whom Jesus chose to be his disciples, while he was on earth, and whom he intended, before going back to heaven, to send out as his apostles, to preach the gospel through the world. Judas was present with Jesus during his whole ministry. He heard all his teachings. He saw all the miracles and wonderful works which Jesus did. And, if he had been a really good man, like Peter or John, he might have spent the years of his life, as they did theirs, in preaching the gospel, and making himself useful wherever he went. But this was not the case with him. He was a covetous man. He let the love of money take possession of his soul,—and this caused his ruin. It led him at last to betray his Master, for thirty pieces of silver. And when he had done this, and began to think about it, he saw the horrible wickedness of his conduct. He felt that this one act had made him the vilest sinner,—the most ungrateful wretch, that ever trod God's earth. This was more than he could stand. Then he went and hanged himself. And whenever we read, or hear, about Judas Iscariot, we may well think of the terrible evil of covetousness. If he had only minded the warning we are considering, how different his life and his death would have been!

We have another Bible illustration of this subject, in the case of Ananias, and Sapphira his wife. We read about them in the fifth chapter of the Acts of the apostles. The day of Pentecost had come, and the Holy Spirit had been poured upon the church. By the first sermon which the apostle Peter preached after this, three thousand persons had been converted. These new converts were so earnest about the cause of Christ, that they sold all the property they had, and gave the money to the apostles, to help on the spread of the gospel.

Among those who joined the church, at that time, were Ananias and Sapphira. But they were not true Christians. Covetousness, or the love of money, was ruling in their hearts. They sold their property too, as the other Christians did, but their covetousness tempted them to try and make some money by the operation. They concluded to keep back part of the price, and pretend that the other part, which they gave to the apostles, was all they had received for the sale of their property. And when the apostle Peter asked them if that was all the money the sale had brought them; they answered deliberately that it was. But Peter knew that it was not so. He solemnly charged them with lying to the Holy Ghost. As soon as he had done this, they fell down dead before him! This was the sad result of covetousness. If it had not been for this, only think what useful lives they might have lived; and how much good they might have done, in helping on the cause of Christ in the world! But their usefulness was all destroyed, and they brought death both on their bodies and their souls, because they did not—"Take heed and beware of covetousness."

I have just one other illustration to give before

leaving this part of our subject. We may call it—

THE LOVE OF MONEY.

This story shows us that when men let covetousness rule them, it makes slaves of them, binding their hearts and minds, and their very souls, with chains which they cannot break, and the effect of which is to destroy all their usefulness.

It is the experience of an old merchant that I am going to give you, who was entirely under the influence of covetousness. He was immensely rich, and had made his money by struggling hard, and by denying himself continually. In speaking about himself one day to a friend, he said—" I must confess that the older I grow, the more I love money, and the less I enjoy it. I am never satisfied unless I have a sum of money at hand, ready for any investment that may offer. My last thought at night, and my first thought in the morning, is about making money. And when I think what it has cost me to make the money I have ; and how happy I might have been—and how much good I might have done, if I had spent more, and been content with less,

I see plainly what a fool I have made of myself, and what a dreary waste my life has been! And still I find that the love of money grows stronger with me every day, and I cannot help it. I feel like an infant in the hands of a mighty giant. I am a perfect slave to the love of money. This feeling will grow worse every day, till the end of life, and then I shall have to give up for others to squander, the money which it has cost me so much labor, anxiety, and unhappiness, to make."

Now it is easy to see how that man's usefulness was all destroyed, by his giving way to the love of money. And it is a good reason why we should "take heed and beware of covetousness," or mind the warning of the text, because if we do not, it will destroy our usefulness.

And the third reason, why we should mind this warning, is—THAT COVETOUSNESS WILL LESSEN, OR LOSE OUR REWARD.

We know how it is with farmers. At the close of the summer, the time for harvest comes. Then they expect to reap their fields, and stow away the crops gathered there in their barns. And intelligent, right-minded farmers, are always very careful not to do anything, that will be likely to lessen, or lose their harvests. They know very well that if they do some things, or neglect to do some others, the effect will be bad upon their harvest. If they should neglect to plow their ground ; if they should not sow the right kind of seed ; or if they should not sow it at the right time, their harvest must suffer from it. Either they will have no harvest at all ; or else it will be poor and unsatisfactory.

Now we are just like farmers, in this respect. The present life is our seed time for eternity,— the time for our plowing and sowing. And the reward, which God promises to those who are faithful in plowing and sowing, is the harvest that awaits us in heaven. And what that reward or harvest will be, must depend entirely on how we are living, and what we are doing now. If we are real Christians, trying to serve God faithfully, and are making a right use of the money he gives us, and of the opportunities of usefulness which He affords us—then we may look for a glorious reward, when our harvest time comes. But, if we are loving money instead of loving God, and are not using our money as God wants us to use it, then we are doing that, which will certainly have the effect of either lessening our reward, or of causing us to lose it altogether. We are making it certain, that our harvest will either be very poor and unsatisfactory, or else that we shall have no harvest at all.

We may find two very good illustrations of this part of our subject, in the teachings of our Saviour. We have one of these in the parable of the talents, in the 25th chapter of St. Matthew.

Here Jesus compares himself to a nobleman, who went into a far country, to receive a kingdom for himself, and then to return. Before going, he called his servants to him, and gave each of them some money, which they were to use for him, while he was gone; and on his return they were to give him an account of what they had done with their money. To one of them he gave ten talents, to another five, and to another two, and then went off on his journey.

In due time the lord of those servants returned. Then they came before him to give an account of what they had been doing during his absence. The first said he had been trading with his lord's money, and had gained ten talents more, than those which had been given to him. His master was very much pleased with this, and gave him a good reward.

Then the second servant came, who had received five talents, and said that in addition to these, he had gained five talents more. His master was well pleased with him, and gave him also a good reward.

Then came the third servant, who had received but two talents. His report was very different from that of the others. He had made no proper use of his master's talents. He had just wrapped them up in a napkin, and kept them near him. It may have been that his love of money was so strong, that when he once had it in his hand, he was unwilling to part with it, either for the sake of doing good to others, or of making more out of it for his master. And so there was no reward for this servant. His talents were taken from him, and he was sent to the place of punishment prepared for the wicked.

And here we see how the love of money, or the wrong use of it, will be sure either to lessen our reward for eternity, or cause us to lose it altogether.

And we have another illustration of this part of our subject, in what our Saviour says in the latter part of the same chapter, the 25th of St. Matthew. Here Jesus is telling about the last judgment. He speaks of Himself, as seated on the great white throne, and all nations as gathered before Him for judgment. They are divided into two great companies. One of these is on His right hand, and the other on His left. He is about to tell each of those great companies, what their portions for eternity would be. He turns first to those on his right hand. They had spent their money in feeding his poor people, when they were hungry,—in clothing them when naked,—and visiting and relieving them when sick and in prison. He told them that in doing this, for any of His people, they were doing it to him. And then He bade them welcome to the glory of His heavenly kingdom. That was their reward. How grand and glorious it was!

Then He turned to those on His left hand. They had never loved or served Him, when on earth. They had been covetous. They had loved their money, and had made a wrong use of it. They had seen His people hungry, yet gave them no bread. They had seen them naked, yet refused to clothe them. They knew of their being sick and in prison, yet never visited them, or did anything for their relief or comfort. And He told them, that in refusing to show kindness to the very least of His people, they had refused to show it unto Him. And then the terrible words which He spoke to them were—"Depart ye cursed into everlasting fire, prepared for the devil and his angels!" How fearful this is! Here we see how the love of money, or the wrong use of it, brought on all those people the entire loss of that reward in heaven which might have been theirs forever.

I have just two other short illustrations of this part of our subject. The first may be called—

NO TREASURE IN HEAVEN.

Two Christian friends called on a wealthy farmer in Illinois, one day, to try and get some money for a charitable work in which they were engaged. He took them up to the cupola, on the top of his house, and showed them farm after farm, stretching far away, on the right hand, and on the left, and told them that all that land belonged to him. Then he took them to another cupola, and showed them great herds of horses, and sheep, and cattle, saying, as he did so—

"Those are all mine too. I came out here a poor boy, and have earned all this property myself."

One of his friends pointed up to heaven, and said—"And how much treasure have you laid up yonder?"

After a pause, he said, as he heaved a sigh, "I'm afraid I haven't got anything there."

"And isn't it a great mistake," said his friend, "that a man of your ability and judgment should spend all your days in laying up so much treasure on earth, and not laying up any in heaven?"

The tears trickled down the farmer's cheeks as he said—"It does look foolish, don't it?"

Soon after this, that farmer died. He left all his property for others to use, and went into the presence of God only to find that his love of money, and the wrong use he had made of it, had caused him to lose all the reward which he might have had in heaven.

Our last story may be called—

TOO HEAVY FOR THE ANGELS.

Some years ago, near Atlanta, in Georgia, there lived a man who was a member of the church. He was a person of some influence in that neighborhood. But he was a covetous man, very fond of money, and always unwilling to pay his debts. He had a little grand-daughter, about nine years old, who was living with him. She was a bright, intelligent young Christian. She had heard of her grandpa's love of money, and his unwillingness to pay his debts, spoken of, and it grieved her very much.

One morning, as they were sitting at breakfast, she said—"Grandpa, I had a dream about you, last night."

"Did you? Well, tell me what it was."

"I dreamed that you died last night. I saw the angels come to take you to heaven. They took you in their arms, and began to go up till they were almost out of sight. Then they stopped, and flew round awhile, but without going any higher. Presently they came down with you, and laid you on the ground, when their leader said—

"'My friend, you are too heavy for us. We can't carry you up to heaven. It's your debts that weigh you down. If you settle with those you owe, we will come for you again before long.'"

The old gentleman was very much touched by this. He saw the danger he was in from his covetousness. He resolved to struggle against it. The first thing after breakfast, he went to his room, and in earnest prayer asked God to forgive his sin, and to help him to overcome it. Then he went out and paid all his debts; and after that was always prompt and punctual in paying what he owed. So he minded the warning of the text, and was kept from losing his reward. Not long after this he really died, and then the angels had no trouble in carrying him up to heaven.

Now we have had three good reasons why we should mind this warning against covetousness. The first reason is, because it will destroy our happiness; the second is, that it will injure our usefulness ; and the third is, that it will lessen or lose our reward.

But we must ask God to help us, and then that which we never could do of ourselves, we shall be able to do, in a way that will be both pleasing to God, and profitable to ourselves.

III.

THE WARNING AGAINST INTEMPERANCE.

"At last it biteth like a serpent, and stingeth like an adder."
PROVERBS xxiii. 32.

HERE Solomon, the wisest of men, compares intemperance to a serpent, that bites, or stings men. Now if there were deadly serpents awaiting us in the paths of our daily life, how important it would be for us to have clear, timely warnings about them, so that we might keep out of their way, and not be stung, or bitten by them!

Some poisonous serpents are only to be found in particular places. We have the rattle-snake in this country, and its bite is often fatal. But in England, and other countries of Europe, it is never found. In Asia they have one of the most poisonous of all serpents, called the Cobra. But we do not have them in our country.

But when we compare intemperance to a serpent, it is one that is not confined to any particular country. We can find it everywhere. And it is one of the most poisonous and deadly of all serpents. Solomon wrote the words of our text—nearly three thousand years ago—to warn us against the evils of intemperance.

Our sermon to-day is about—

THE WARNING AGAINST INTEMPERANCE.

This is the most dangerous of all serpents. And there are three things, about the sting of this serpent, which should lead us to mind the warning here given.

In the first place we should mind this warning against the serpent of intemperance, because, its sting is—a costly sting.

If you are bitten by some other serpent, it may give you pain for a little while, but you can soon get medicine to cure the bite, and that will be the end of it. But it is very different with this serpent of intemperance. O, how much the bite of this serpent costs! Let us look at some good illustrations of this part of our subject. Our first story may be called—

AN OLD MAN'S EXPERIENCE.

One day, a gentleman in London, was taking his favorite walk near Regent's Park. As he went on his way, he saw an old man sitting to rest under the shadow of a tree, by the roadside. He knew, from his dress, that he was one of the inmates of the neighboring Alms-house. The gentleman stopped to talk with him, when the following conversation took place between them.

"What a pity it is, my friend," said the gentleman, "that a man of your age, should have to spend the rest of your days in the Poor House. May I ask how old you are?"

"Close on to eighty years, sir."

"What was your trade?"

"I was a carpenter, sir."

"Well, that's a good trade, to get a living by. Now let me ask you plainly, were you in the habit of taking intoxicating liquors?"

"No, sir;—that is, I only took my beer, three times a day, as the rest of the men did. But I never was a drunkard, if that's what you mean."

"No, I don't mean that; but I should like to

THE WARNING AGAINST INTEMPERANCE. 63

know how much a day your beer cost you?"

"Well, I suppose it was about sixpence a day."

"And how long, speaking freely, do you suppose you continued to drink it, in that moderate way?"

"Why, I suppose, about sixty years."

Then the gentleman took out his pencil, while the old man went on talking about his temperate habits, and the misfortunes that had overtaken him. When the gentleman had worked out his sum, he said to the old man:

"My friend, temperate as you say your habits have been, let me tell you that your sixpence a day, for sixty years, at compound interest, has cost you the sum of three thousand two hundred and twenty-six pounds sterling. (That would be sixteen thousand, one hundred and thirty dollars of our money.) And if instead of spending that money for drink, you had laid it aside for your old age, you might now, in place of living in a poor-house, and being dressed as a pauper, have an income of one hundred and fifty pounds, or seven hundred and fifty dollars a year. That would give you three pounds, or fifteen dollars a week, for your support." Surely that old man found the sting of this serpent a costly sting!

Our next illustration may be called—

A GALLON OF WHISKEY.

At the end of a certain week, a set of eight or ten workmen all had their wages paid to them. Instead of going home with their money, they went to the tavern together. They each agreed to pay as much money as would be needed to buy a gallon of whiskey. They bought it. Then they concluded to have, as one of them said— "a jolly good time." They drank it all up. This made them all more or less drunk. And now, let me tell you what that gallon of whiskey cost. I do not mean by this how much money the men paid for it, but how much misery and trouble was occasioned by it.

As that company of drunken men were on their way home that night, four of their number got into a quarrel. The quarrel ended in a fight. The result of that fight was that two of them were killed. The two men who killed them, were tried, and sentenced to prison for fifteen years. Now think of all this. There were two men murdered : two more condemned to prison, perhaps for the rest of their lives. Then there were four poor wives left as widows ; and twelve children left without a father to support them, or to take care of them. How dreadful to think of what that gallon of whiskey cost!

Our next story may be called—

ONE GLASS OF RUM.

A temperance meeting was once being held, in a sea-port town in New England. In the course of the meeting, a sea-captain rose, and asked to be permitted to say a few words. He was requested to say all that he desired.

"My friends," said he, "I wish to tell you what a single glass of rum once cost me. I had a small vessel, that used to go on voyages along the coast. On one occasion I took my wife, and our two little children with me, for the benefit of a sea voyage. One night during that voyage, we had quite a severe storm. My brother was the mate of the vessel. After my watch was over that night, I left my brother on deck, to keep watch, and have charge of the vessel while I was asleep.

Two of the sailors persuaded him to take a glass of rum. He was not in the habit of drinking intoxicating liquors. It overcame him, and he fell into a deep sleep. I was awakened, about midnight, by a heavy shock. Hurrying upon deck, I found that the vessel had been dashed against the rocks, and was a complete wreck. I took my wife, and one of my little ones, in my arms, and she took the other in hers. And then, for hours, we were struggling desperately with the cold stormy waves. After awhile a heavy wave swept over me, and carried my wife, and my darling little one, from my embrace. The same wave swept the other child from the arms of my wife. Thus both our little ones were lost for ever. I then turned to try and help my dear wife. But just as I did so, she gave up the struggle, and sank from sight in the deep waters. Then I made my way to the shore, with my heart almost broken, as I said to myself—'There is my wife—my two children—my vessel, and its cargo—all swept away as the cost of—one glass of rum."

May we not well say that the sting of this serpent is a costly sting?

Our next illustration is not a story, but some very surprising—

FACTS ABOUT INTEMPERANCE.

The amount of intoxicating liquors, used in the United States, in one year, would fill a canal four feet deep, fourteen feet wide, and one hundred and twenty miles in length. How costly that would be!

If all the liquor saloons, and hotels, of New York city, were placed in opposite rows, they would make a street, like Broadway, eleven miles in length.

The places in which intoxicating liquors are made, and sold in this country, if placed in direct lines, would make a street one hundred miles in length. Think what all those miles of property would cost!

If the drunkards of America were placed in ranks, five abreast, like an army, they would form a procession a hundred miles in length! And if we should stand by, and watch that great army of drunkards, as they marched along, more than half a million strong, going on to sure and swift destruction, we should see, that all who left the ranks of that vast army, were taken either to the poor-houses, the prisons, or the gallows; and yet their ranks are constantly filled up by the moderate drinkers. And as we think of the march of that great army, who can tell about the fortunes wasted—the hopes crushed—the hearts broken—and the homes made desolate by drunkenness? Surely the bite of this serpent is a costly bite!

Our next illustration may be called—

A CHILD'S ANSWER.

A little boy had attended a temperance meeting one night. When he came home his father said to him—" Well, my son, have you learned anything to-night?"

" Yes, I have, father."

" Well, what is it you have learned?"

" Why, I have learned never to put any strong drink to my lips; for they say that intemperance is killing half a million of persons every year, and how do I know but it may kill me? so I have made up my mind to have nothing to do with it." That is a good lesson for any boy or girl to learn.

When we speak of losses in connection with drinking, we generally think only of those which the drunkard meets with, as the result of his intemperance. But here is an incident which brings out the other side of this matter. We may call it—

WHAT A MAN LOST BY NOT DRINKING.

A man who had signed the pledge, was attending a temperance meeting one evening. After hearing a great deal that had been said, about the losses caused by intemperance, he rose to make a short speech.

"My friends," said he, "I have heard a great deal about the losses which follow from drinking, but no one has said a word, about the losses which come from *not* drinking. I wish to speak a little on this point, and tell you something about my losses, since I signed the pledge not to drink any more. Listen, and you will soon see what I mean."

The other day there was a nice job of work to be done, in our shop, requiring very careful management. I heard the boss call out—
'Give that job to Law, he is the best hand in the

shop.' I finished the job, and when I went home that night, I told my wife about it.

"Why, Lawrie," said she, "the boss used to call you the worst hand in the shop. You've lost your bad name, haven't you, since you signed the pledge?"

"That's a fact, wife," says I, "but that isn't all I've lost since then. I used to have poverty and wretchedness, and I've lost them. I used to have an old ragged coat, and a shocking bad hat, and some India-rubber boots, that let the water out at the toe, as fast as they took it in at the heel. I've lost *them.* I used to have a red face, and a trembling hand, and a pair of shaky legs, that gave me an awkward tumble every now and then. I've lost them. I used to have a bad habit of cursing and swearing, and I have lost that. I used to have an aching head sometimes, and a heavy heart, and worse than all the rest— a guilty conscience; but now, thank God—I've lost them all!"

"And then I told my wife what *she* had lost."

"Mary," said 1, "you used to have an old ragged gown; but you've lost that. And you used to have trouble and sorrow, and a poor wretched home, and plenty of heartaches, for you had a miserable drunkard for a husband, and you have lost all them! O Mary! Mary! thank the Lord, for all that you and I have lost, since I signed the pledge!"

Now I wish to finish this part of our subject by asking your attention to what we may call—

THE PYRAMID OF INTEMPERANCE.

I met with this, some years ago, in one of our religious papers. I was very much interested in it, and thought it would be useful to illustrate the point we are now considering—the cost of Intemperance. In this pyramid, we have a comparison made between the amount of money paid for liquor in a year, and the amount paid for ten other, of the principal things made use of, in the carrying on of life in our country. If you look at the lowest step in this pyramid, you will see that the cost of liquor is $900,000,000 a year. And then you can climb up the pyramid, step by step, and compare the cost of liquor with that of the other things mentioned.

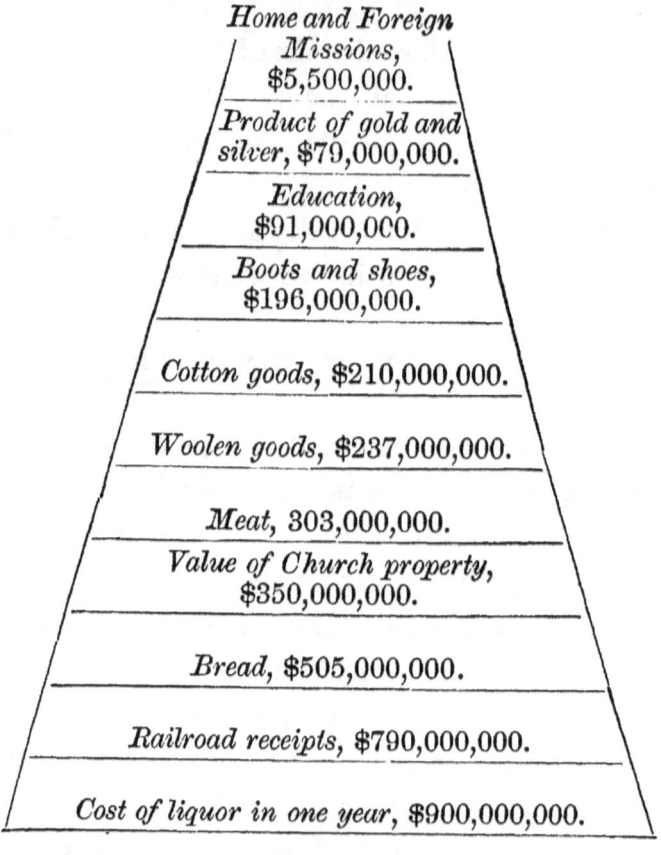

And so, after all that has been said on this subject, we see how well we may mind the warning, which Solomon gives us, about this serpent of intemperance, because its sting is so costly.

THE WARNING AGAINST INTEMPERANCE. 73

In the second place we should mind this warning against the serpent of intemperance—because its sting is—an INJURIOUS STING.

The bite of a serpent is never pleasant. It will often cause pain and inflammation, but these effects can generally be removed. They are not always injurious. But how different it is with the terrible serpent of intemperance! Who can tell all the fearful injury that is done by its sting? I wish now to tell you something about this injury. Listen to these illustrations. The first may be called—

A HEART-BROKEN WIFE'S INJURY.

One cold wintry day, a poor woman went to a wood yard. Going up to the man who kept it, she held out a piece of money to him and said: —" Sir, can you let me have a quarter of a cord of wood for this? It's all I've got in the world, and my children are freezing."

The man looked closely at her, for a moment or two, and then said—

"Why, arn't you the wife of Seth Blake, the lawyer?"

"Yes, sir, I am," said the woman.

"Then pray tell me, my friend, how you ever came to be so poor?"

"Drink did it all, sir," answered Mrs. Blake.

"That's bad," said the man.

"Yes, sir, it is bad," said the woman. "My children are starving, and drink did that. My children are ragged, and drink did that. My children are growing up outside of the Church, or the Sabbath school, and the week-day school, and drink did that. My husband, once a kind, respectable, and prosperous lawyer, is now a poor, cruel, worthless vagabond, and drink did that. My heart is breaking, sir. The joy of my life is gone, and drink has done it all." And then the poor woman sat down upon a log of wood, and wept bitter tears—the very picture of want and woe.

How terrible that serpent must be, whose bite can cause such injury as this!

Our next illustration may be called—

A WHOLE FAMILY DESTROYED BY DRINK.

This story occurred in connection with my own ministry in this city.

Some years ago, I had an interesting family

belonging to my parish. The family consisted of a mother, the widow of a sea-captain, with her daughter and son. The daughter was a bright, intelligent Christian girl. She was, for several years, a teacher in my Sunday-school. Then she was taken with some disease of the spine, which confined her to her bed, for years in great suffering. The mother was also an invalid, and could only go from her own room to her daughter's, by being moved in a large arm-chair, on wheels.

The son was a promising young man, with excellent business talents. At one time he had a situation, in one of our largest mercantile houses, with a salary of $2000 a year. He had an encouraging prospect before him, of becoming one of our first merchants. But he was bitten by this terrible serpent. He learned to drink. Then he soon lost his situation.

After this, he got into the habit of spending his evenings in a drinking saloon, not far from his mother's house. At the close of the evening he would be too drunk to walk, and some of his companions would carry him home, lay him on the steps, and ring the bell, for the servant to come and take him in.

One night, he was not quite so drunk as usual. He refused to be carried on that occasion, and said he could walk himself. He managed to stagger home. But, in trying to get up the steps of his mother's house, he stumbled and fell. In falling he struck his forehead against the corner of one of the marble steps, and received a severe wound. He was carried up into his mother's room, and laid upon her bed. The shock of seeing her poor son's bleeding form, was too much for her. She fainted at the sight, and died, within twenty-four hours, from the effect of the shock. Her son was carried to the Hospital, and died about the same time that his mother did. I buried them both together in the same grave. It was the saddest funeral I ever attended.

This double stroke of affliction, falling on that poor sick daughter and sister, was too much for her. It unsettled her mind. Within a few days after the funeral, she thought some one was trying to get into her room to injure her. In her alarm, she sprang from the bed—opened the window of her room, which was in the second story, and leaped out of it. She fell upon the pavement, and was killed! Thus a *whole family* was destroyed by the sting of this terrible serpent. May we not well say, that it is an *injurious* sting?

Not long after this, while walking one day, by the drinking saloon, which had caused all this misery, a gentleman, connected with the family, said to me :—"Dr. N——, if you take that saloon as a centre, and draw a circle around it, with a line that would take in two squares, on every side, I could point you to not less than 20 families, within that circle, on which the blighting influence of that one drinking saloon has come down in some form of fearful evil." O, certainly, the sting which produces such sad results as these, may well be called—an injurious sting!

Our next illustration may be called—

A YOUNG MAN'S SAD STORY.

A gentleman was travelling from Boston to Albany, in the cars. At one of the stations, a fine looking young man entered the car, and sat down by his side. They soon got into conversation together, and talked on a variety of subjects. It seemed that the young man was a theological student, and was about to enter the ministry. Something was said about the drinking customs of the day. This caused the young man to say to his companion—

"Sir, I am only 25 years old; and yet you can't tell me anything new about intemperance. I know it, all through, to my sorrow."

"Please tell me your story," said the gentleman. And then he gave the following account of his experience:—"When I was eighteen years of age, I went to Boston, to have charge of the books in a large mercantile house. At my boarding-house I became acquainted with four young men, who were clerks like myself. They were in the habit of drinking beer and ale, but nothing stronger then. They invited me to join them in drinking, but I declined. They pressed their invitations very earnestly. I said, 'I have never drunk a glass of liquor in my life, and I do not intend to begin now. It would not be just to my temperate parents, nor to my Christian home.'

"Now it happened so that one of those young men had a great turn for fun and ridicule. He said things that made the others laugh at me. This was more than I could stand. I finally yielded and drank the first glass of intoxicating liquor, that had ever crossed my lips. The habit grew upon me. I soon became a drunkard, and lost my situation. In two years I had an attack of delirium tremens, and found myself standing on the very brink of a drunkard's grave, and of a drunkard's hell. I was greatly alarmed. Then I resolved, by the help of God, to break away from that terrible slavery. I solemnly vowed, never again to taste a drop of intoxicating liquor. God helped me in that struggle. I became a sober man and a Christian. And here I am to-day, a brand plucked from the burning, and soon to go forth and preach the glorious gospel of the Son of God."

"And what became of those four young men, who urged you to drink?" asked his companion.

"Three of them are now filling drunkards' graves; and the fourth is in the state prison of Vermont for life. But for the grace of God, I might have been in the grave with the three, or in prison with the fourth!"—Certainly that young man's story proves that the sting of this serpent is an injurious sting.

I have just one other illustration, of this part of our subject. We may call it—

THE WIDOW'S CURSE.

Mrs. Faulkner, was a good Christian widow in Connecticut. She had an only son, who was getting on very well in business, till he became intemperate. This almost broke his mother's heart. She wept, and pleaded earnestly with him, to quit drinking. At last he agreed to sign the pledge, to the delight of his mother. Soon after this, he told her that the temptations about him there, were so great that he would have to go away from home:—" but mother dear, you may depend upon it, that with the help of God, I will keep my pledge."

He went away, but she continued to hear good news from him. When he had been gone a little over two years, she received a letter from him one day, saying,—" Mother, I am coming home to spend Thanksgiving-day with you."

How happy that made his mother! She resolved to prepare for him the best dinner in her power.

He came into the town by stage—for this was before the days of railways. The stage stopped at the door of Solomon Perkins' tavern. The young man got out there. Several of his old companions were standing round the door. "Holloa, Fred!"—they cried—"how are you? And what'll you have to drink?"

"Nothing, thank you."

"What, not at Thanksgiving time? Come, take a little."

"No, I'd rather not. I've come home to see my mother. She hardly expects me to-night. I thought I'd wait till dark, and then go in and surprise the old lady."

Just then, Solomon Perkins, the keeper of the tavern, looked at him and said—

"Fred Faulkner, if I were six feet tall, and broad in proportion, as you are, and yet was afraid of a paltry glass of ale, I'd go to the woods and hang myself."

"But I'm not afraid," said the young man.

"Oh, yes you are—ha, ha, ha! I say, boys,

here's a *great big fellow*, afraid of a glass of liquor. I suppose he's afraid of *his mother*."

Then they all laughed at him. This was more than he could bear. They handed him a glass of liquor, and dared him to drink it.

"Well," said he, "I'm going to my mother, and I may as well show you that I am not afraid of a glass of liquor."

He drank it. Then his old taste for liquor revived in him. He went on drinking. By midnight he was so drunk, that he could neither walk nor stand. They carried him to the barn, and left him there all night, on a heap of straw. In the morning, when they went to look for him —they *found him dead!* How awful to think of!

They carried him to his mother, stretched on a plank, with a buffalo robe thrown over his body. O, think of the anguish of that poor mother's heart! and of the deep distress into which she was plunged for all the rest of her life!

Perkins the tavern-keeper, called on the sorrowing mother the next day. As soon as she saw him she said—"Perkins, why did you tempt my boy to drink?"

"I didn't know it was your son."

"O, yes, you called him by name. You knew it was Frederick Faulkner, the only son of his poor crippled mother. *You knew it, and you have killed him.*"

And then, laying one hand on the body of her dead son, she stretched out the finger of her other hand, and shaking it at the miserable man who had brought down this crushing load of grief upon her, she said, in startling tones:—
"*May the curse of God follow you all your days!*"

For all the gold and silver of the world, a thousand times over, I would not have been in that man's place!

Could anything show, more strikingly than this incident does,—how terribly injurious the sting of this serpent is?

I will close this part of our subject, with some impressive lines, which show us, when men are allowed to sell intoxicating liquors, what it is they are licensed to do. They are—

>"*Licensed* to make the strong man weak,
> *Licensed* to bring the good man low;
> *Licensed* the wife's fond heart to break,
> And make the children's tears to flow.

Licensed to do thy neighbor harm,
   Licensed to kindle hate and strife;
Licensed to nerve the robber's arm,
   Licensed to whet the murderer's knife.

Licensed thy neighbor's purse to drain,
   And turn his feast into a fast;
Licensed to heat his feverish brain
   Till madness crowns his work at last.

Licensed, where peace and quiet dwell
   To bring disease, and want, and woe;
Licensed to make this world a hell,
   And fit men for a hell below."

The second reason why we should mind this warning against the serpent of intemperance is because its sting is injurious.

But then the sting of this serpent is—A DISGRACEFUL STING—and this is the *third* reason, why *we should mind this warning against it.*

We never think of such a thing as disgrace, in connection with the bite of any other serpent. It may cause us pain and uneasiness. We may consider ourselves as unfortunate to be so bitten; but the idea of disgrace, or dishonor, in connection with any stings we may happen to have, never enters our minds. But it is very different, with the sting of this terrible serpent of intemperance. Those who are bitten by it, are all the time doing things that are foolish and disgraceful.

Let us look at some illustrations of the different ways in which this is done. Our first incident may be called—

PLAYING DRUNK.

This story is told of a physician, who had been very successful in his profession, and had quite a large practice. But he had allowed himself to get into the habit of drinking, and would often go staggering home quite drunk. One day, after dinner, he was lying on the sofa, and his two little boys were playing in the same room. As he lay there, not asleep, but with his eyes half closed, he heard his boys talking together in their play.

One of them said to the other, "Come, let's play drunk, and stagger about as papa does when he comes home."

Then the elder boy began the play. He went reeling and staggering about the room, rolling his head from shoulder to shoulder, speaking in a thick, rough voice, and imitating his father's drunken ways. As the father lay there, seeing and hearing all this, his eyes filled with tears, and his heart with grief. "Is it possible," he said to himself, "that I, an educated, and intelligent man, and occupying so important a place in society, should allow myself to act in a way so perfectly ridiculous, and disgraceful, before my family and friends? My boys shall never see me act so foolishly again. From this day forward, as long as I live, by the help of God, I'll never take another drink of intoxicating liquor." And he was true to his promise. It was a profitable play which those little boys had that afternoon, in showing their father the disgrace of intemperance.

Our next story is one that was told by a prominent Methodist clergyman in England. We may call it—

ONLY ONCE DRUNK.

"I never shall forget," says this good minister, "the end of one with whom I was acquainted, and who was for years a member of my church. He had been a moderate drinker all his days, but had never been known to be intoxicated. On one occasion, he had some important business, with a merchant from another city, who was accustomed to drink very freely. He invited my friend to spend the evening with him at the hotel, and attend to their business. They were drinking from time to time, all through the evening. For the first time in his life my friend became intoxicated. At the close of the evening he went home drunk, and excited by liquor, not knowing what he did, he struck his wife a severe blow, which caused her death. He was arrested and put in prison. When the trial came on he was found guilty, and the sentence of death was pronounced against him. I visited him in his cell," says his minister. "I went with him to the scaffold, offered the last prayer with him, and stood by to see him executed; and there, within sight of the church, of which he had been for more than twenty years a member, he was hung like a dog! I never shall forget that scene." Here we see how disgraceful the sting of this serpent is!

I have only one other illustration of this part of our subject. It was written by an earnest, intelligent friend of the temperance cause. He wished to show the disgrace which the drunkard leaves, to all connected with him, when he dies. So he wrote out what he called—

THE DRUNKARD'S WILL.

It represents one who has been bitten by this dreadful serpent. He is looking forward to the day of his death; and this is what he says:

" I die a wretched sinner, and leave to those behind me, a dishonored reputation, a wicked example, and a memory full of disgrace.

I leave to my parents, sorrow, and bitterness of soul, all the days of their lives.

I leave to my brothers, and sisters, shame and grief, and the reproach of their acquaintances.

I leave to my broken-hearted wife, and widow, a life of lonely struggle, with want and suffering.

I leave to my children, a dishonored name, and the mortifying recollection of a father, who by his life disgraced humanity; who died before his time, and went to join the company of those who never can enter the kingdom of God. May those yet living take warning, and profit

THE WARNING AGAINST INTEMPERANCE. 89

by the reading of this my last will and testament."

And now, let us look back over what we have been speaking about. Remember where our text is: Prov. xxiii. 32. Remember the words of the text: "At last it biteth like a serpent, and stingeth like an adder." Remember what our sermon is about: the warning against intemperance. Remember to what intemperance is here compared, to a serpent. And remember, the *three* things about the sting of this serpent, of which we have spoken. It is a *costly* sting,—*an injurious* sting,—and a *disgraceful* sting.

I will close our subject, in the way of application, by quoting some very appropriate lines, which some one has written on this subject. They are intended to show us what we should do, whenever we are tempted to drink intoxicating liquor. They are headed—

DARE TO SAY—"NO."

Dare to say "No," when you're tempted to drink;
Pause for a moment, my dear friends, and think—
Think of the wrecks upon life's ocean tossed,
By answering—"Yes"—without counting the cost;

Think of the mother who bore you in pain!
Think of her tears, that will fall like the rain;
Think of her heart, and how cruel the blow,
Think of her love, and at once answer—"No!"
Think of the hopes that are drowned in the bowl;
Think of the danger to body and soul;
Think of sad lives that were white as the snow:
Look at them now, and at once answer—"No."
Think of a manhood with rum-tainted breath,
Think how the glass leads to sorrow and death;
Think of the homes, that now shadowed with woe,
Might still have been happy, and firmly say—"No."
Think of lone graves, both unwept, and unknown,
Hiding fond hopes that were fair as your own;
Think of proud forms now forever laid low,
That still might be here, had they learned to say—"No."
Think of the serpent that lurks in the bowl,
The serpent of ruin to body and soul;
Think of all this as life's journey you go,
And when you are urged by the tempter—say—"No."

IV.

THE WARNING AGAINST THE TRANSGRESSOR'S WAY.

"*The way of transgressors is hard.*"—PROVERBS xiii. 15.

A TRANSGRESSOR means a sinner. To transgress means to walk over. God's commands are like the lines which mark out the paths that He desires us to walk in. But when we break God's commands, we walk over or tread under foot, the lines which mark out the way in which we ought to walk. And this makes us transgressors, or sinners. And in our text, Solomon tells us what sort of a way it is that we walk in, when we do this. He says,—" The way of transgressors is hard."

How many different kinds of ways, or paths, we find to walk in, here in this world! There is the walk through the garden, in the spring, when the flowers are blooming around. There is the walk along the ocean's shore, when the beautiful surf is rolling up. There is the walk over the fields, on a summer evening; or through the woods in autumn, when the leaves are changing their color, and every prospect pleases. What easy and pleasant ways these are to walk in! But there are other paths, very different from these.

If the path you have to walk in, lies over a hot and sandy desert, or if it leads you up the steep side of a mountain, or over sharp rugged rocks, or slippery ice, then we may well say that such ways as these are hard to walk in. But the way of transgressors is harder than any of these.

Our sermon to-day, is about *the warning against the transgressor's ways.*

Solomon says his way is hard; and there are *four* losses, caused by transgression, which help to make this way hard, and which should lead us to mind this warning.

*The first thing, that helps to make the way of the transgressor hard, is the loss—of a good conscience—*which follows from it.

What is conscience? Conscience is something, which God has put in our hearts, or minds, to encourage us to do what is right, and to warn us against doing what is wrong. It has a voice, which we may well think of as the voice of God, that speaks to our souls. And our happiness or misery, depends very much on the way in which this voice of conscience speaks to us. When we do what is right, conscience speaks pleasantly to us, and that makes us feel comfortable and happy. But when we do what is wrong, conscience finds fault with us, and reproves us, and we cannot help feeling unhappy when this is the case.

And so one of the things which helps to make the way of transgressors hard, is the voice of conscience, when it is made uneasy, on account of the wrong things that we have done. This was what Solomon meant when he said—"The spirit of a man will sustain his infirmity—but a wounded spirit"—or the voice of an uneasy, or guilty conscience—"*who can bear?*"

We have a good illustration of this part of our subject, in the case of Judas Iscariot. Shortly after he had betrayed his master, Our Blessed Saviour, he went and hanged himself. Now why did he do this? He had nothing to fear, in the way of punishment, from the Jewish rulers. Nobody would have hurt him, for what he had done. Then why did he go and hang himself? It was because of the trouble which his conscience gave him, for what he had done. If you and I had been near Judas then, and could have listened to the voice of his conscience, we should have heard it saying to him something like this:—"You are a vile and miserable wretch! You have done the basest, and the wickedest thing that ever a man did. You are not fit to live. Every one who sees you will despise you, and point the finger of scorn at you!"

This was more than Judas could stand. Who *could* stand this? We do not wonder, that under these circumstances, Judas did go and hang himself. And as we think of his dead body, hanging on the tree, what a striking illustration we have here—that—"The way of transgressors *is* hard."

I have one other illustration here. We may call it—

A SAILOR'S SAD EXPERIENCE.

This sailor was the captain of a large mer-

chant ship. In one of his voyages, he came in sight of a vessel that had been wrecked, in mid-ocean, and was in a sinking condition. He saw the signals of distress, and heard the shrieks of the men and women crowding the decks; but he kept on his course, and would not stop. The officers and crew implored him to stop, and offered, at the risk of their own lives, to try and save the poor creatures from the sinking ship. But the captain would not listen to them. This was very unlike what true sailors are. They are generally unselfish, and ready, at any risk, to help those who are in trouble. And what led that captain to act in this selfish and cruel way? Let me tell you. It was the love of money. His vessel was loaded with a very costly cargo. At the port for which he was sailing, the goods he had on board were in great demand, and brought a very high price. Another vessel had sailed the same day, from the port he had left, laden with the same kind of cargo, and going to the same port. The captain felt sure that if he reached port, before the other vessel, he would certainly make enormous profits.

So he sailed on his course, and left the crew

and passengers, clinging to that wrecked vessel, go down in the deep waters, unhelped. Before the end of the voyage, he got each person on board the ship, to promise never to tell about the loss of that wrecked vessel, and he rewarded them for doing so. Then he reached port several days before the other vessel. He became very rich from the sale of his cargo; but he lived and died a miserable man. He never could forget that sinking wreck, and the poor creatures who went down with it. The thought of it tortured him by day, and occupied his dreams by night. He had a splendid house by the sea-side, but when the storms swept by, he fancied he could hear, in the wail of the winds, the wild shrieks of the men and women whom he might have saved, but did not. Sometimes he would start from his sleep, giving out the command—"Lower the boat,"—only to find the cold sweat of agony on his brow, and to feel his tortured conscience gnawing like a serpent at his heart. He found that "The way of transgressors is hard." And the first thing that makes it so, is the loss of a good conscience.

The second thing that makes the way of the trans-

gressor hard is—THE LOSS OF CHARACTER—*which follows from it.*

We see how this was, in the case of Adam and Eve. When God created them they were pure and holy beings. Their characters were perfect. God placed them in that beautiful garden of Eden, which He had prepared for them. There, they had everything they could desire to make them happy. God was their Father and Friend, and the angels were their companions. They could walk about that lovely garden, and eat of the fruit of all the trees that grew there, except *one*. That was called—"the tree of the knowledge of good and evil." God had told them that they must not eat of the fruit of *that* tree. *This* was the only commandment which God gave them. Now surely they might have been willing to obey this one command, and let *that* tree alone. If they had only done this, they never would have lost the good character which they then had, and they might have lived in Paradise all their days. But Satan found his way into that garden. He tempted them to break that command. They ate of the fruit of the tree, which God had said they must not eat. Then they lost their character, as good and holy beings, and were driven out of that lovely garden, never to enter it again. And as they went out, poor miserable sinners, though they had never heard these words of Solomon, they must have felt—that "The way of transgressors is hard."

The loss of character made it a hard way to them. And this is what it will always do. Now let us look at some other illustrations of this part of our subject.

The first one may be called—

THE EFFECT OF ONE SIN.

A letter carrier in one of our large cities, found, on reaching the post-office—after going round his beat, a letter at the bottom of his bag, which he had failed to deliver. He ought to have gone right back, at once, and delivered that letter. But he was tired and hungry. He thought it was only an ordinary letter, of no particular importance, so he thrust it into his pocket, to be delivered the next day. Thus he failed of doing his duty. *This* was his transgression.

And what was the result of this neglected act of duty? For want of that letter, a great firm failed to meet their engagements; their notes were protested; a large mill was closed, and hundreds of poor workmen were thrown out of employment.

And what was the effect on the letter carrier himself? He lost his character. He was discharged from his office, and his family suffered all through that winter, for want of the necessities of life. Surely *he* found—"the way of transgressors was hard!"

Our next story may be called—

THE FIRST STEP IN THE TRANSGRESSOR'S WAY.

A young man was once sent to prison for stealing $20,000 from the merchant whose clerk he had been. As he sat in the loneliness of his miserable cell, the first evening of his confinement, he could not help thinking over what he had done. And as he was doing this,—the question that pressed itself upon his mind was— "*How came I here?* People will say, it was cheating my employer of that large sum of money. But that is a mistake. It was something before that. I look back twenty years. I remember, one bright summer day, when my good old uncle John, sent me to the country store, to pay a bill for him. I got the bill receipted, and seventy-two cents were given me as change. On my way home I said to myself, 'If uncle asks me for the change, of course I'll give it to him; but if he doesn't ask me, I guess I'll keep it.' I kept thinking about this all the way back. My conscience told me what was the right thing for me to do. But the tempter said to me—'Well, what's the use of giving them back? If your uncle doesn't ask for them, you might as well keep them.' I made up my mind to do this. My uncle did not ask for the pennies, and *I never gave them back to him. That was my first step* in the transgressor's ways. It was cheating my uncle out of those seventy-two cents, which ruined my character; and now here, in this gloomy prison, I must find out how hard the way of transgressors is!'

And thus we see that the second thing which makes the way of transgressors hard, is the loss of character which follows from it.

The third thing which makes the way of the transgressors hard, is—THE LOSS OF USEFULNESS—resulting from it.

It is a very hard thing to have our ability for usefulness taken away from us. Here is a good illustration of what I mean. Suppose we have before us a mariner's compass. It is a round box, about six inches wide, with a glass cover over it. If we look into this box, we see at the bottom, a sheet of white paper, that fits closely into it. On the surface of this paper, we see a circular ring printed, with east, and west, and north, and south, and all the points of the compass marked on it. In the middle of the box, is a smooth piece of steel, in the shape of a flat needle. It is fixed on the point of an upright piece of iron, so that it can easily turn round in any direction. God has given to that needle the power of pointing to the north, at all times, and in all places. This is a wonderful power. We call it magnetism. We do not know what it is. But it is this power, which that little needle has, of turning to the north, which makes the mariner's compass so useful. The sailor takes it with him, as he sails over the ocean, and thus he is able to steer his vessel, in the right direction, wherever he may be. But if any thing could be done which would take away from that little needle the power which it has of turning to the north,—then, all its usefulness would be gone. It would no longer do the sailor any good. He would not care to take it with him any more.

And what the magnetism of that little needle, or its power of turning to the north, is to the mariner's compass,—the power of making ourselves useful is to us. If people know that we are trying to do right;—if they are sure that we are honest, and true, *then*, there is no telling what good we may do, and how useful we may be. But, if we do what is wrong; if we allow ourselves to go in the way of transgressors,—then we lose our character, and that must take away very much our power of being useful.

Here are some illustrations of this part of our subject. The first may be called—

"IF I HAD ONLY DONE MY DUTY."

Some years ago a man became insane, from the accusations of his conscience, for having neglected his duty. He had been a watchman on a railroad bridge in Connecticut. When at his post, the duty expected of him was to throw up a signal light, when the draw in the bridge was open, so that trains coming along, might see it in time to stop, before reaching the opening in the bridge. One dark night, he allowed himself to fall asleep, instead of going out, and hoisting the signal, in time to give warning to any train that might be coming along.

Presently an express train came rushing by. No signal light was seen. That train did not stop; but on it pushed, till it plunged into that opening in the bridge. There was an awful wreck. A great number of unfortunate persons were crushed to death; and many more were fearfully wounded.

When the guilty watchman was searched for the next day, it was found that the thought of the terrible evil he had done, had made him crazy,—and all that he could say was—"*Oh! that I had only done my duty!*" With a frightful look he muttered these words over and over again. After this, the remaining years of his life were spent in an insane asylum; but every day, till the day of his death, he was heard repeating the same sad words—"Oh! that I had only done my duty!" Surely that poor man found the way of transgressors a hard way.

Our next story may be called.

USEFULNESS HINDERED.

A Christian merchant, in one of our large cities, said to a friend one day—" I wonder why it is that none of my clerks have become Christians, and joined the church?" "If you will allow me to speak plainly on this subject," said his friend, "I can show you where the difficulty lies." "By all means," said the merchant,— " speak as plainly as you please."

" Well then," said his friend, "you know that you have a very violent temper. You often speak sharply to your clerks, and find fault with them, when they are really not to blame. This leads them to doubt the reality of your religion, and interferes with your usefulness.

The merchant was not offended with his friend, for he felt that what he said was true, and thanked him for his plain speaking.

On reaching home that night, he went to his room, and kneeling down there, he confessed his sin to God, with bitter tears, and prayed for forgiveness. Then he asked God to help him to overcome his bad temper, and to be gentle and kind, as Jesus was.

On going to his place of business, the next morning, he called all the clerks into his office. With tears streaming down his cheeks, he told them how sorry he was, to think of the bad temper he had often shown before them. He asked their forgiveness for having spoken crossly to them, and said that he wanted to tread in "the blessed steps" of his Saviour's life, and to have the same mind that was in Him. Then he kneeled down and prayed with them.

After that, none of those young men ever saw any more bad· temper, on the part of that merchant, and before long, more than half their number, influenced by his good example, became Christians, and joined the church. Now this merchant went into the transgressor's way, when he let his bad temper overcome him; and he found it was a hard way, because he lost his usefulness by it, and could do no good to the young men in his employment. And so, the third reason why the way of transgressors is hard, is because of the loss of usefulness—to which it leads.

But there is a fourth thing that makes the way of transgressors hard, and that is—THE LOSS OF THE SOUL.

It is quite possible for any transgressor to save his soul, and get to heaven. The greatest transgressor that ever trod the earth, if he will only repent, and believe in Jesus, may find his way to heaven. We know very well that— "when Jesus had overcome the sharpness of death, he opened the kingdom of heaven to all believers." But, when we go into the way of transgressors, we do not know that we shall ever have an opportunity of repenting, and believing in Jesus. And *then*, no matter what part of the transgressors' way we may have walked in, we shall find it a hard way,—because it will be sure to bring the loss of heaven to us. And if we lose heaven, the only thing that can remain for us will be—*everlasting punishment.* And *that* must be a hard way to walk in, which is likely to lead to such an end as this.

Let us look at some illustrations of this part of our subject. The first one may be called—

DUTY NEGLECTED.

This story relates to a family who were very well off. But the father and mother of this family never went to church, and never said a word to their children on the subject of religion. One of their sons was sick, with the consumption; but they would not tell him that he was likely soon to die, nor allow any one to speak to him on the subject. They tried to be cheerful and merry before him. They did everything in their power to keep up his spirits, and to prevent him from thinking of the great change that was soon to overtake him. But at last, they saw that death was near. His father and mother, and brothers and sisters, could no longer hide their feelings from him. He saw them sitting, or standing round his bed, in tears. He could not tell what it meant.

"What's the matter with you all?" he exclaimed. But they were all silent. And then the terrible thought came into his mind of what was going to happen to him. "Am I in danger? Am I *dying?*" he asked, in great alarm. They dared not,—they could not deny it. They only wept in silence round his bed. "Then I am lost!" he screamed out. "Lost! There *is* a hell. I feel it. I am *in* it. And you—*you*," he cried, turning a look of agony upon his parents—" are the cause of the loss of my soul." And then he died. How dreadful that was! Who would want to have stood in the place of those sorrowful parents? They had gone in the way of trnsgressors, by neglecting their duty to God, and their duty to their children. How hard it must have been for them to think that their transgression, in the way just spoken of, had brought on the son they loved so much—the loss of his soul! And yet it was just so.

I have one other illustration of this part of our subject. We may call it—

A TOUCHING STORY.

In a seaport town on the west coast of England, some years ago, notice was given of a sermon to be preached one Sunday evening, on the proper observance of the Sabbath. The minister, who was to preach on this occasion, was very eloquent, and a large congregation met to hear him. After the usual service was over, and the hymn sung, the minister gave out his text, and was about to begin his sermon, when he suddenly paused, leaned his head on his hand, and rested his elbow on the pulpit, and remained silent for a few moments. Some of his friends were afraid that he was feeling unwell. But he soon straightened himself up, and looking round on the congregation, he said: "My friends, before beginning my sermon, I ask your kind indulgence while I relate to you a short anecdote."

"It is now fifteen years since I was last within this place of worship. The minister who preached on that occasion, was the beloved and venerable man who was then the pastor of this church. The subject of the discourse that night, was the same that has brought us together this evening—the proper observance of the Sabbath. Among those who came to the church, that evening, were three young men. They were wild, ungodly, drinking men, who were already far gone in the way of transgressors, and who came that night, not only for the purpose of insulting and mocking the venerable pastor, but with stones in their pockets, to throw at him, as he stood in this pulpit."

"The minister had not gone on very far with his sermon, when one of the young men said to his companions,—'What's the use of listening to the old fool any longer? Let's throw now.' But the second one stopped him, saying—'Let's see first, what he is going to make out of the point of the sermon which he has just begun.' But the young man's curiosity was soon satisfied, and he said: 'O, confound him! it's all nonsense, just as I expected. Let's throw now!' But the third one of their company then said: 'Boys, I think we had better give up altogether, the bad intention which brought us here.' On hearing this, his companions were greatly offended, and immediately left the church, while he remained till the close of the service. Those two young men went on in the way of transgressors, while their companion made up his mind to stop, and not walk in that way any longer."

" And now, my friends," continued the minister, with great feeling, "let me tell you about the after history of those three young men. Of the two who left the church that night, one was hanged several years ago at Tyburn, for the crime of forgery; the other was lately hung for murder. They died with the burden of their sins still upon them, and thus they lost their souls; the third "—and here the speaker's voice failed. He was greatly agitated, and paused awhile to wipe away the big tear-drops from his face—"the third, is he who is now about to address you—listen to him."

This is indeed a touching story. Those two young men went on in the transgressors' way, and it brought on them these four terrible losses—the loss of a good conscience—the loss of character—the loss of usefulness—and the loss of the soul. And this must be the case with all who keep on walking in this way.

Now remember where our text is to-day—Proverbs xiii. 15. Remember what the words of the text are:—"The way of transgressors is hard." Remember what the sermon is about,—the warning against the transgressors' way. And remember the *four* losses which help to make this way hard:—The first is the loss of a good conscience; the second is the loss of character; the third is the loss of usefulness; and the fourth the loss of the soul. And let us all ask God to give us grace to keep out of the transgressor's way. And if any of us are still walking in that way, like the third of those young men of whom we have just spoken, let us resolve, by the help of God, to stop, and not walk in that way any longer. I will close this sermon with some very suitable lines which are headed—

"IT'S NEVER TOO LATE TO MEND."

A word with you! remember this,
   And comfort take, my friend—
That though you may have done amiss,
   "It's never too late to mend."

Your present course, day after day,
   Would to your ruin tend,
But you can stop that downward way,
   "It's never too late to mend."

Though Satan has you in his power
   You can defeat his end,
For even at the eleventh hour,
   "It's never too late to mend."

> God heeds repentance, if it's right,
>   And blessings shall descend
> Upon thy head, for in His sight
>   "It's never too late to mend."
>
> And many now in peace above,
>   Might well this message send—
> A warning unto those they love,
>   "It's never too late to mend."

But wherever you go, and whatever you do, always remember these solemn words—

THE WAY OF TRANSGRESSORS IS HARD.

V.

THE BIBLE WARNING AGAINST LYING.

Lying lips are an abomination unto the Lord.—Proverbs xii. 22.

It is surprising how much the Bible has to say about the proper use of our tongues. The apostle James tells us, that if we only learn to manage our tongues in the right way, it will make us perfect. He tells us how we are able to control our horses, by means of the small bits which we put into their mouths, and how we are able to turn about our largest ships, by means of the little helms or rudders, which we fasten in their sterns. And so he tells us that if we only manage to control our tongues in the right way, we shall be able to regulate our whole bodies.

Now one of the very worst ways in which the tongue can be used is, when it is made to say what is not true, or, in other words, to tell lies.

And the subject of our sermon to-day is—*the Bible warning against lying.* I wish to speak of *three* reasons, why we ought to mind this warning.

We ought to mind this warning against lying—*In the first place because of*—WHAT GOD THINKS ABOUT IT.

There is hardly any form of wickedness, against which God has spoken so often, and so strongly in the Bible, as He has against lying. He says, in one place,—"The mouth of them that speak lies shall be stopped." In another place he says—"A lying tongue is but for a moment;" and in yet another,—"He that speaketh lies shall perish."

There is no greater honor to be found anywhere, than they will have who are permitted to enter heaven, and see God's face, and live with Him. But how terrible it is to hear God say,—"He that telleth lies shall not tarry in my sight." In another place God says—"I hate and abhor lying." But in our text, we have one of the strongest passages which the Bible gives us, to show what God thinks about lying. Here we are told that—"Lying lips are an abomination unto the Lord." Who would want to be considered as an abomination, by that great, and good, and holy Being, who sits upon the throne of heaven; and whom all the angels of heaven, love, and honor, and praise, and worship? This ought to lead each of us to take our stand here, and say:—" Well, whatever else I may do, by the help of God I am resolved that I will never tell a lie, because that will make me an abomination unto the Lord."

To know what God thinks about lying should lead us to mind the warning against it. And now let us look at some illustrations, of the influence which this thought has had, in keeping persons from lying.

Our first story may be called—

THE FIRST AND ONLY LIE.

This story is told of a little boy named Willie. He was only about six years old, and was a dear good boy, very much beloved by his family, and all who knew him. Willie's father had a violin, which he often used to play, for the amusement of his children in the evening.

On one occasion, a neighbor of theirs whose name was Taylor, borrowed this violin, and kept it for a long time. At breakfast time one

THE WARNING AGAINST LYING. 117

morning, Willie heard his father say that he wished Mr. Taylor would send his violin back.

When Willie and his brother John, a little older than himself, were coming home from school that afternoon, he said,—"Johnnie, let us go round by Mr. Taylor's and get papa's violin." So they went. When they came near the house, they met Mr. Taylor. Willie went up to him and said,—"Mr. Taylor, papa sent me to get his violin." "All right," said Mr. Taylor, "I'll send it round this evening."

Now notice, if Willie had simply told Mr. Taylor that his father wanted to have the violin back again, it would have been all right. But his father had not sent him to get it; and when Willie said he had, he did not tell the truth. "After we left Mr Taylor's," said his brother Johnnie, in speaking of it afterwards—"I noticed that Willie was very silent, and seemed troubled about something. I could not tell what was the matter. At last he started, and ran towards home. When I got there, I found him with his face buried in mother's lap, sobbing and crying as if his heart would break. Mother asked me what was the matter. I was telling her that we had been to Mr. Taylor's about father's violin—when Willie looked up, and said, as the tears rolled down his cheeks—"I told a lie—I told a lie!" and then he went on sobbing as before. Pretty soon he went over to a corner of the room, and kneeled down. With his hands clasped, and the tears streaming down his cheeks, he confessed his sin unto God, and prayed earnestly to be forgiven. And what was it which made that dear boy feel so badly on account of the untruth which he had spoken? It was just the thought that his lying would make him an abomination unto the Lord. He felt that he never could have a moment's peace, till he was sure of God's forgiveness. About a year after this, the dear boy was taken sick, and died a very happy death. *That*—was Willie's first and only lie. If he had lived to be a hundred years old, he never would have told another lie. He would always have remembered what God thinks about lying. And this would have led him to mind the warning against this sin.

Our next story may be called—

THE INK SPOT, OR THE TRUTHFUL BOY.

Charley Jones, and his sister Lizzie came home from school one afternoon, early in January. Charley was about eight years old, and Lizzie was six. After putting away their overclothes and school books, they concluded to go into their father's library, and have a good time in looking over the beautiful books, on the centre table, which had been sent to him as Christmas presents. They had great pleasure, in opening one book after another, and looking at the nice engravings, which were in them. For some time every thing went on pleasantly; but after awhile, they both happened to lay their hand on one book at the same time, and each wanted to have it.

"Let me look at it first, Lizzie," said Charley, "because I'm the oldest."

"No," said Lizzie, "I got hold of it before you did. So you must let me see it first."

"No, I wont," said Charley, and then a struggle began between them, in which each tried to get the first use of the book. While this struggle was going on, the book got pushed off the table, and fell to the floor. At the same time an inkstand was knocked off the table, and all the ink in it was poured out on that beautiful book. The children were frightened when they saw this. There was that great terrible ink-mark, which spoiled the beauty of the book. And what was to be done now? The children looked at each other; and then they looked at that ugly stain on the book. It was getting late, and they knew that their father would soon be home. "O, what shall we do?" asked Charley, in great distress. "Indeed, I don't know," said Lizzie.

"I'll tell you what I'll do," said Charley. "I'll put that book away down under all the others. Then father wont see it to-night, and if after some days, he sees that ugly stain, he'll think that one of the girls did it, while fixing up his library. That will be the best thing to do."

Charley was going on to carry out his plan, when suddenly he stopped. He looked down on the floor, evidently thinking seriously about something; and as he did so, he turned very pale. What was the matter with him? Why he remembered just then, that at family prayers

THE WARNING AGAINST LYING.   121

that morning, after reading the Bible, his father said;—that " God is with us in all places. He sees everything we do, and hears everything we say; and if we say what is not true with our lips, or do what is not true in our actions, He will be angry with us, and we shall be an abomination unto Him."

Charley reminded his sister of what their father had said that morning. And then he said:— " No, Lizzie, I can't think of trying to hide this from father. I'll tell him honestly, and truly, all about it. I can bear to have him scold me, or even whip me, but I can never bear to do what is not honest, and true, because *that* will make God angry with me."

When his father came home, Charley told him what he had done, and asked his forgiveness, with many sobs and tears. His father was so pleased to find that his little boy had honestly spoken the truth about it, that he only told him to try and be more careful another time, and then he kissed him, and forgave him. And here we see how the thing which made little Charley afraid of doing, or saying what was not true,— was the remembrance of what God thinks about it. And so we ought to mind the Bible warning against lying, because of what God thinks about it.

And then, the second reason why we ought to mind the Bible warning against lying is, because of—WHAT MEN THINK OF IT.

Between three and four hundred years before Christ, there was a famous philosopher in Greece, whose name was Aristotle. He was the teacher of that celebrated General—Alexander the Great. Aristotle was a very wise man. Somebody asked him, one day, what a man could gain by lying. The reply of the philosopher was:—"his gain will be this, that no one will believe him when he speaks the truth."

We are told that there was a distinguished poet in Italy, whose name was Petrarch. This man had gained for himself a well-known character for speaking the truth. On one occasion he had to appear in court, as a witness in a certain trial. In such cases it is customary, before a witness is allowed to speak, for one of the officers of the court, to get him to take a solemn oath, in which he pledges himself to speak—"the truth, the whole truth, and nothing but the truth." But when the officer was about to get Petrarch to take this oath, the judge rose in his place, and said—"Never mind, sir. It is not necessary for Petrarch to take that oath; for every one knows that he never speaks anything but what is true."

That, was an honorable character for any one to have. And these incidents show us clearly, what men think about lying; and how highly those persons are esteemed, who gain for themselves the reputation of always speaking the truth.

In the country of Siam, in Asia, we are told that a person who tells a lie, is punished according to law, by having his mouth sewed up. If this law prevailed in our country, and was faithfully carried out, in going through the crowded streets, how many people we should see with their mouths sewed up!

These incidents throw light on the point of our subject now before us, and show us clearly what men think about lying. And now, let us look at some other illustrations of the same kind.

The first may be called—

"I ALLUS KEEP MY WORD."

Mrs. Woodward was a lady, who lived in a nice house, on the turnpike road, about half a mile from a large village in England. At the close of a stormy day in March, she was sitting by the window of her house, wishing that some little boy would come along. Her husband was absent from home, and she was expecting a letter from him, and she wanted some one to go and get it for her. Just then she saw a ragged little fellow going along the road, whistling. She rapped at the window, and the boy stopped. Opening the window she said, " Here, my little man, don't you want to earn something this evening?"

"What do you want me to do, marm?" asked the boy.

"I want you to go to the post-office, and ask for a letter for Mrs. Woodward; and if you bring it safely to me, I'll give you two shillings. Will you go?"

"I guess I will, marm," said the boy; "shillinses don't grow on every bush; and especially in this cold weather. Will yer gi'e the money now, marm?"

"I would if I was sure I could trust you. Will you be sure to bring me the letter?"

"I said I would, marm, and I allus keeps my word," said the boy, straightening himself up proudly, and looking the lady full in the face.

Mrs. Woodward took out her purse, and gave the boy two shillings. His eyes sparkled with delight, under the ragged brim of his hat; and saying—"Thankee, marm," with great glee, he made an awkward bow, and the next minute he was out of sight.

This took place between five and six o'clock. Then Mrs. Woodward had her tea, and after that she took her seat in front of the fire, waiting for the boy to bring her letter. But she had a long time to wait. The clock struck seven, but no boy came. It struck eight, and nine, and still the boy did not come. Then she blamed herself for giving the boy the money, before he brought her the letter. But about half-past nine, just as she was thinking of going to bed, there came a loud knock at the kitchen door. Bridget jumped up and opened it, and there was the boy. "Well, you really did come back," said Mrs. Woodward.

"I said I would, marm, and I allus keeps my word. I never tells a lie," exclaimed the boy. "I've got the letter in my pocket, marm. Will yer please get it out?" he said, turning to Bridget, "for I'm stiff with cold, yer see, and most frozen," and his teeth chattered as he spoke.

Mrs. Woodward gave him a seat by the fire, and told Bridget to get him a cup of warm tea, and some nice things to eat, while she went into the next room to read her letter.

When she came back he had finished his supper, and was feeling very comfortable, as he sat by the warm fire.

"I am very much obliged to you for bringing me the letter," said Mrs. Woodward, "but what kept you so long?"

He did not seem willing to answer her at first. But she pressed him to tell her, and he said at last, as the tears were running down his cheeks, "Ye see, marm, it was my little sister that I was trying to help. She got hurted inside some time back. It was drink did it. Poor father didn't mean to hurt her. But when he came home drunk one night, he gin her a push, and she fell over the stove. And the doctor says she wont never get no better ; and she has the fever on her all the time, and she's allus a hungerin' arter oringes, and lemmins, and sich sour things, to cool her mouth. But they cost so much, an' mother can't more'n git along with her washin', and so ye see, I was glad to git a chance to take poor Jess what she was a cravin' for, so she might go to sleep easy. That was what I axed the money for, and gitten them things for Jess is what took me so long."

Mrs. Woodward was moved to tears by the poor boy's touching story. And when he was getting ready to go, she said—" No, my little man, you mustn't venture out in this storm again to-night. Bridget will make up a bed for you, in the loft over the kitchen. You can sleep comfortably there, and in the morning, after breakfast, I will go home with you, and see what I can do for your poor sister. And when Mr. Woodward comes back, I'll tell him about you, and ask him if he can't give you something to do in his store; for I know he would like very much to have a boy about him, who can truly say—

'I allus keep my word.'" The little fellow went to bed feeling very happy that night. The next morning Mrs Woodward went home with Robbie, for that was the boy's name, and did everything in her power to make little Jessie comfortable. When Mr. Woodward came back, he was very much interested in what his wife told him about Robbie. So he took him into his store as errand boy. He was so industrious and reliable, that before long he was raised to a higher position; and finally he became head clerk of the firm. After his poor sister, and his drunken father were dead, and buried, he was able to support his mother comfortably, as long as she lived. All this good came out of that boy's minding the warning against lying, and his being able to say—"*I allus keep my word.*"

Here is a short illustration which may be called—

LYING WORSE THAN STEALING.

A little girl came to her mother, before breakfast one morning, saying, " Mamma, tell me what you think ; which is the worst, lying or stealing ? " Indeed, I hardly know, my dear.

They are both very bad. I hope you wont have anything to do with either of them."

"Well," said the little girl, "I've been thinking a great deal about it, and I've come to the conclusion that it's worse to lie than to steal. For you see, if you steal anything, when you are sorry for what you have done, you can take it back, unless it's something you have eaten, and even then you can go and pay for it; but "—and then there was a look of awe in the little girl's face—as she said, "if it's a lie—it is there forever!"

The last illustration, of this part of our subject, may be called—

WHAT AN ENGLISH NOBLEMAN THOUGHT OF LYING.

The person here referred to was the famous Algernon Sidney. He lived in the troublesome times of King Charles I. It was common then, for men to be imprisoned and even put to death, simply because they held different opinions, on some political matters, from those which were held by the heads of the government.

Sidney had written a political paper, and signed his name to it. The king was greatly offended by this paper. He ordered him to be arrested, and put in prison. He was afterwards tried, and condemned to death, for what he had written. That paper was brought to him in prison. His attention was called to the signature attached to the article, and he was told, that if he was willing to say that he had not signed that paper, his life would be spared, and he would be released from prison. Now here you see, the great question, which Algernon Sidney had to settle was this—" Shall I tell a lie and save my life, or shall I tell the truth and lose it ?" His answer was—" I did sign that paper. I could save my life by telling a lie, but I would rather a thousand times tell the truth, even though my life must be the cost." That was noble ; and so the second reason why we should mind the Bible warning against lying is, because of what men think of it.

The third reason, why we should mind this warning is, because of—THE PUNISHMENT WHICH MUST FOLLOW LYING, AFTER DEATH.

Whatever the effect of our lying may be in this life, it will soon be over. But the consequences of lying, which must follow us after death, will last forever. Let us look for a moment, at two passages of scripture, which show us very clearly, what the consequence of lying will be after death, so that we never should forget them.

One of these passages we find in Rev. xxi. 27. Here, the apostle John is giving his beautiful description of that glorious heaven, which Jesus has prepared for those who love and serve him, and he tells us that—"there shall in no wise enter into it anything that—"*maketh a lie.*" Whenever you are tempted to tell a lie, think about this passage, and say—if I allow myself to tell lies, I never can enter heaven, when I die. And then, in the 8th verse of this same chapter, we are told that—"all liars shall have their part in the lake which burneth with fire and brimstone." There is something awful in these words. How earnest the recollection of them should make us, in trying to mind the Bible warning against lying! Whenever you are tempted to lie, think of those terrible words, and then say to yourself—"if I give way to this temptation, instead of going to heaven when I die, I must find my place forever, in that awful lake which burneth with fire and brimstone.

Now let us look at one or two illustrations, which show us how the thought of the punishment, which must follow lying after death, will help to keep us from committing this sin.

Our first incident is very short, but just to the point. We may call it—

AFRAID OF LYING.

One day, a little boy had been sent on an errand by his uncle. He had stopped several times on his way, to watch the boys playing marbles, and to look at the store windows; but at last he remembered how long he had been gone, and then he started to run back to his uncle's work-shop, as fast as he could go.

When he got near the shop, he met one of the workmen, who said to him—

"Why are you running yourself out of breath, in that way, Charley? Just tell your uncle that the people kept you waiting."

"But the people didn't do it," said Charley, "and that would be a lie."

"To be sure it would, but what difference would that make?"

"I a liar? I tell a lie!" said Charley, indignantly. "No, not if it was to escape a whipping every day. My mother always told me that lying was the first step to ruin. I want, above all things, to go to heaven when I die, but my Bible tells me that no liar can enter heaven."

I have one other story, to illustrate this part of our subject; we may call it—

KEPT FROM LYING BY FEAR OF THE FUTURE.

This story was told by an English merchant, who had been very successful in his business. In talking to a friend one day, he said—"When I was fifteen years old, I was in the service of Mr. C., a farmer in Yorkshire. One day Mr. C. was expecting a gentleman from a distance, to buy one of his horses. That animal had certain defects, which, if the gentleman intending to purchase it knew about, he would not be willing to take it. Mr. C. said to me,—"Now, Bob, if this gentleman should ask you, whether the horse has any defects, you must be sure and say, No, sir. Do you hear?" "Yes, sir, I hear, but

I can't do that. I know the horse *has* defects, and I can't tell a lie about it. I never told a lie in my life, and I am not willing to begin now." This made Mr. C. very angry.

"Well," said he, "if you don't do as I tell you, I'll give you such a horse-whipping as you'll never forget while you live."

My answer to him was—"Sir, I can stand the horse-whipping; but the Bible tells me, that—'all liars must have their part in the lake of fire,' and *that*, is something that I cannot stand. So my mind is made up never to tell a lie."

Just after this, the gentleman on horseback made his appearance, and began bargaining for the horse, for which he offered quite a large sum. He asked a number of questions, about certain defects, which horses sometimes have, and he wanted to know if this horse had any of those defects. Mr. C. assured him, positively, that he hadn't one of them. And then, to confirm what he had said, he called on me, and began to ask me, in the presence of the gentleman, if the horse was not perfectly sound? In answer to this, I said at once—"No, it isn't." "What!" exclaimed the gentleman, "isn't it sound?" "No, sir, it isn't, and Mr. C. knows that as well as I do." Then the gentleman was much offended, and gave the farmer a severe rebuke, and declared that he would neither buy that horse of him, nor any other, as long as he lived.

No sooner had he departed, than Mr. C. followed me to the stable where I had gone. He shut the door, and taking a large horse-whip, he laid it on me most unmercifully, till my back and shoulders were black and blue. "And now," said he, "you'll know better than to disobey me another time."

When he was going out of the stable, as I was smarting from the cruel lashes of that whip, I called out after him—"Satan is preparing a warm place for you in that lake of fire."

And now, see what took place immediately after this. The farmer went towards a large water trough, in the barn-yard, where the horses used to go to drink. As he was standing there, a frisky young horse came by. Raising himself on his front feet, he jerked out his hind feet with great violence, and struck Mr. C. a heavy blow on the head. He fell to the ground, insensible.

He never rallied from that blow, and died before the next morning. Who would want to be in that man's place, and to bear the punishment for lying, that would follow him after death? The thought of that punishment, is a very strong reason, why we should mind the Bible warning against lying.

And now let us remember where our text is to-day. Proverbs xii. 22. Let us remember the words of the text: "Lying lips are an abomination unto the Lord." Let us remember what the sermon is about: it is the Bible warning against lying. Let us remember the reasons given, for minding this warning. These are how many? Three. We ought to mind this warning in the first place, why? Because of what God thinks about it. We ought to mind this warning in the second place, why? Because of what men think about it. And then we ought to mind this warning in the third place, why? Because of the punishment which must follow lying after death.

These are three very good reasons why we should resolve never to tell a lie. And let our daily prayer be, that God would help us to set a watch at the door of our lips, and to be careful, at all times, to speak only the words of truth and soberness.

> "May peace guard our lives, and ever
> From the time of our early youth,
> May the words we daily utter
> Be the words of beautiful truth!"

VI.

THE WARNING AGAINST SIN.

'Be sure your sin will find you out.''
NUMBERS xxxii. 23.

ONE thing which has much to do with leading people to commit sin, is the thought that they can do it in secret, and not be found out. Many a boy is tempted to play truant, instead of going to school, because he thinks that his father and mother will never know anything about it. Many a robber breaks into a house at night, and steals what he wants, because he thinks that no one sees him, and so his sin will never be found out. But here in our text, we have a warning against sin because it is sure to be found out. And there are three things for us to remember, which help to make it sure, and should lead us to mind this warning.

And the first thing, which must make it sure that sin will be found out, is—THE PRESENCE OF GOD.

This is something from which we can never

THE WARNING AGAINST SIN. 139

get away. David was feeling this, when he wrote the 139th Psalm. Here he asks—"Whither shall I go from thy Spirit? or whither shall I flee from thy presence? If I ascend up into heaven, thou art there; if I make my bed in hell, behold thou art there. If I take the wings of the morning, and dwell in the uttermost parts of the sea; even *there*, shall thy hand lead me, and thy right hand shall hold me." Solomon says—"The eyes of the Lord are in every place, beholding the evil and the good." Prov. xv. 3. If we could only remember these four words—" Thou God seest me "—it would be a great help to us in minding the warning we are now considering, and in keeping us from committing sin. The thing that tempts us to commit sin more than anything else, is forgetting that God is looking at us, all the time

Now let us look at some illustrations, of this part of our subject. The first may be called—

YOU ARE WATCHED.

In refitting the old Post-office, in New York, some years ago, the carpenters who did the work, were surprised to find that there was a sort of private gallery, all round the walls of the large room, in which the principal work of the office was done. In the walls about that room were a great number of tiny holes, and at each of these holes a person was stationed, whose business it was to keep a careful watch over the persons at work in the room. They were watched all the time, though they did not know it. If one of them should attempt to open a letter, which had money in it, and steal that money, some one of those watchful eyes would see it. The person seeing it, would report to those in authority, what had taken place. Then the thief would be called out of the office. He would be handed over to a policeman, and sent to prison.

So his sin would be found out, because he was so faithfully watched. But those Post-office workmen are not the only persons who are watched, when they do not know it. Those about us are watching us. The angels are watching us. Yes, and more than that, the Lord of the angels is watching us. When men watch us, it is not certain that they will always see everything that we do. Sometimes they may be called away; or their eyes may be turned in another direction, and then they cannot see what we do. But it is different with God—our Heavenly Watcher. He is called—" *The All-seeing God.*" His eyes are in every place, beholding the evil and the good. There is no spot in all the world, or in all the universe, where He is not always present ; and He never sleeps, or slumbers. His eye is never closed. In the words of the hymn, we well may ask here—

> " Amidst the deepest shades of night
>   Can there be one who knows my way?
> Yes, God is as a shining light,
>   That turns the darkness into day.
>
> " When every eye around me sleeps,
>   May I not sin without control ?
> No ;—for a constant watch He keeps,
>   O'er every thought, of every soul."

Surely this thought should lead us to mind the Bible warning against sin !

Here is another illustration. We may call it—

THE BANKER'S STORY.

A Christian gentleman, who lived near a large city, had a son about 19 or 20 years of age. The father was anxious to obtain for his son a situation in one of the banks in the city. After having made many efforts, he finally succeeded in obtaining for him just such a position as he desired. On returning home at the close of that day, he told his son about it, and said, that on the following Monday he would take him into town, and introduce him to the president of the bank, and then he could begin his work. "And now, my dear boy,"—said his father—"I want you to be obedient, obliging, civil and respectful, to all who are about you. You have now to form your character for life, and to lay the foundation for your fortune. Be very attentive to your business; and above all, remember the text that has so long hung on your chamber wall—'Thou God seest me.'"

He thanked his father for the good advice he had given him, and promised to follow it. He began his work earnestly, and kept on with it faithfully. The officers of the bank all thought a great deal of him. He rose by degrees from one position to another, till he became the head clerk in the bank. The key of the fire-proof closet, in which the money and valuable papers

THE WARNING AGAINST SIN. 143

of the bank were kept, was left in his charge. It was his duty before leaving the bank at the close of the day, to see that all the money was safely put away, and the fire-proof carefully locked up.

One day, a friend of this young man's told him that he knew of an opportunity of investing $5000, in a way that was entirely safe, and by which he would be sure to make a good deal of money.

The young man thanked his friend, but said he hadn't got that much money, and so he could not take advantage of this opportunity. But, after his friend was gone, Satan came and tempted him. He suggested to him that he might take $5000 out of the bank, when no one was there, and so he would never be found out. At first he resisted this temptation; but after struggling against it for awhile, he gave way to it, and made up his mind that he would take this money.

Now this young man's mother was an earnest Christian. And when her boy was growing up, she tried every way, to fix in his mind, the thought that God was present with him in every place.

To help her in doing this, she got a big card, on which was printed, in large letters, beautifully illustrated, this short text:—" Thou God seest me." This was hung up in his bed-room, so that he might see it the last thing at night, and the first thing in the morning.

Well, at the close of the day, of which we are speaking, when he was left alone in the bank, before leaving, he went into the fire-proof closet, and picked up a parcel containing $5000 in notes, which he intended to take away with him. But he had no sooner taken hold of the parcel, than, in a moment, that illustrated text, in his chamber, came into his mind, and it seemed as if an angel's voice was saying to him,—"Thou God seest me." Instantly the parcel fell from his hands. He sank to the floor on his knees, and clasping his hands, exclaimed with great earnestness—"O, my mother's God! save me from this great sin." God heard his prayer, and helped him. He rose from his knees; put back the money; locked all up and went out.

The first thing he did after this, was to go to the president of the bank. He told him frankly all about it; and then asked to be dismissed.

The president was a wise and good man. He said—" No, my young friend, you keep your position. The thought of God's presence which has kept you from sinning now, will always keep you from sinning. You go on doing your duty, as you have done, and all will be right. I will never say a word about this to any one."

" Be sure your sin will find you out." The first thing that makes this sure is—THE PRESENCE OF GOD.

The second thing which makes it sure that sin will be found out, is—THE POWER OF GOD.

Men often try to do things, but are obliged to give up, because they have not the power, which is necessary for doing them. You know for how many years, the different nations of the world—England, our own country—Germany and Russia, have been trying to get up to the north pole; but they have never succeeded in doing it. All their efforts have been in vain. They have not the power to get there. But it is very different with God. *He* has all power in heaven and on earth. Nothing is impossible for Him to do. He has the hearts of all men in His hands, and He can turn them as the rivers of water are turned. He can do according to His own will, in the armies of heaven, and among the inhabitants of earth.

And so, when He says to us—"Be sure your sin will find you out," we know very well, that He has power enough to bring about this result. The angels of heaven serve Him. And suns, and moons, and stars, and seasons, and day and night, and all things serve Him. His power controls them all. He has determined that every sin, committed by any of His creatures, shall be found out. And nothing is more sure, or certain, than that this will be done, in every case. Now let us look at some illustrations of the different ways in which God's power works to find out the sins of His creatures. Our first story may be called—

THE SINNER FOUND OUT.

"I was walking along the Strand in London, one day," said a gentleman to a friend, "when I saw a policeman go up to a young man, and lay his hand upon his shoulder, saying as he did so—'I want you.' "The young man turned very white," said the gentleman. "There was a startled, frightened look in his eyes, but he made no resistance, and as he walked off with the officer, I heard him say, 'I thought it would come to this; it's just what I expected.'"

On making further inquiries about him, this gentleman found out that the short, sad story of that young man was this :—He was the son of respectable parents. After serving his apprenticeship, with a carpenter in the village where he lived, he came to London, seeking for work. He found employment in a large shop, where he received good wages, and for a while he was getting on nicely. Unhappily he made the acquaintance of some bad companions. They taught him to drink, and to gamble, and to spend his money very foolishly. Before long he found himself heavily in debt. One day, the counting-house clerk being absent, this young man was sent to the bank, to get a check cashed, for a large amount of money. Then the thought came into his mind—" If I keep this money I can soon get out of debt." And then, instead of going back to the shop, he kept the money, and went off with it. He was afraid to go home, or show himself among his friends. He went to another part of London, and prowled about the little streets and alleys, feeling very wretched and miserable, and afraid of being seen by any one that knew him. Several policemen were put upon his track, and had his appearance described to them, and this was one of them who found him. He was tried for stealing, found guilty, and sent to prison. It was the power of God, which caused this young man to be found out in his sin, and that power is able to find out every sin. That young man's sin was found out for its punishment. But sometimes God's power leads to the finding out of sin for its pardon. Our next story will illustrate this. It shows us—

HOW A LITTLE GIRL'S SIN WAS FOUND OUT.

One day, a minister was preaching from the words of our present text—" Be sure your sin will find you out." He said many solemn things about sin finding out those who commit it. Among other things he said this: " If you do not find out your sin, and bring it to Jesus to get it pardoned, and washed away through His blood; you may be sure that your sin will find you out, and bring you to the judgment seat, and the Judge will send you away into everlasting punishment."

Now it happened that there was a little girl in church that day, who had told her mother a lie before leaving home. As she sat listening to the minister's words, she said to herself: " O that terrible lie! I must either find it out, and bring it to Jesus, or it will find me out at the last day, and bring me to punishment."

The poor child was greatly alarmed. She became very anxious about her soul's salvation. She could not think of anything else. She hardly slept any all that night. The next day, she made up her mind to go to her minister, and talk with him about all she felt and feared. She had to walk several miles to reach his home. Then she told him all about her trouble, and ended by saying—" O, sir, what shall I do with my sin ? " "There is only one thing to do with it, my child," said the minister, " and that is to lay it on— 'the Lamb of God who taketh away the sins of the world.'" Then he kneeled down with the poor child, and asked the blessed Saviour to pardon her sin, and comfort her heart, and give her the help of His grace, to keep her from sinning in this way any more.

The little girl went home feeling greatly relieved. The next time she saw the minister, she went up to him with a bright and happy face, and thanked him for teaching her how to lay her sins on Jesus. "I feel very happy now," she said, "and I don't think I shall ever tell another lie as long as I live."

Here we see how the power of God found out that little girl's sin, in order that she might get it pardoned.

I have one other story under this part of our subject. We may call it—

A SECRET MURDER FOUND OUT.

A man who worked on a farm in the State of Connecticut, murdered the owner of the farm, one night, in the stable near the farmer's dwelling. Then he robbed the farmer's house of all the money, and the valuable things to be found in it. After this he left that part of the country, and went abroad. He remained away for twenty years. A large reward was offered for the apprehension of the murderer, and a particular description of his person, was published in the newspapers, to aid in finding him. But of course, as he had gone immediately out of the country, he could not be found.

But now, I wish you to notice, in what I am going to say, how singularly the Providence and power of God worked together to have this man's sin found out at last.

On coming to his old neighborhood after twenty years' absence, he supposed, of course, that the murder, and all about it, would be forgotten; and so it was. But God had not forgotten it; and see how strangely He caused it to be found out. On arriving in his old neighborhood, the man took a walk, so that he could look around and see what changes had taken place. As he was walking, it began to rain heavily. He sought shelter from the rain, by going into a tavern, which stood near the old farm, on which he used to work.

The tavern had changed hands, and all the persons about it were strangers to him. As he stood by the open fire, drying his wet clothes, another man, who had also been out in the rain, stood by him, drying his clothes too. They had a few words of conversation together. Then this other man went to the window, and looked out, to see if it was likely to continue raining much longer, as he wished to go on his way. Now it happened, that one of the panes of glass in that window, had been broken. To keep out the cold air, a piece of an old newspaper had been pasted over it. This newspaper was 20 years old. As the man stood there, and looked at that paper, he read an account of a murder, which had been committed in that neighborhood. A large reward was offered to the person who should find the murderer. Then a description was given of the personal appearance of the murderer, and special mention was made of a peculiar mark, which he had on his face. This startled the man very much. He read the article over again, very carefully. Then he said to himself—"That man standing by the fire, yonder, must be this murderer." Then he walked quietly back to the fire, and looked at the man again. He became satisfied that he was right. Then he asked the keeper of the tavern to go with him into another room. As soon as they were alone, he told him of his suspicions. A constable was sent for.

THE WARNING AGAINST SIN. 153

The man was arrested, and taken to prison. In due time he was tried,—found guilty,—and hung.

How wonderfully God's power operated to find out that murderer's sin, and to bring on him the punishment which he deserved! And here we see that the second thing which makes it sure that sin will be found out—is the power of God.

And the third thing, which makes it sure that sin will be found out—IS THE PURPOSE OF GOD.

What this purpose is we are plainly told by Solomon, when he says that,—" God will bring every work into judgment, with every secret thing, whether it be good, or whether it be evil." Eccles. xii. 14. This purpose makes it absolutely sure, that every sin which is committed, will certainly be found out, sooner or later. Men's purposes do not amount to much, because they are not always able to carry them out. But it is very different with God. He says Himself,— " *My purpose shall stand,* and I will do all my pleasure." Men's opposition to God's purposes amounts to nothing. It was the purpose of God that the children of Israel should be delivered from their house of bondage in Egypt, and go to live in the good land which He had promised them.

Pharaoh refused to let them go, and used all the power of his kingdom, to keep them still in bondage. But by the simple waving of the rod of Moses, all Pharaoh's efforts were made useless, and God's purpose was carried out. So it always *has* been, and so it always *will* be. And this is what makes it so sure, that sooner, or later, every sin will be found out. Let us look at some illustrations of the different ways in which this may be done. Sometimes sin is found out in the very act of its being committed. We see this illustrated in an incident which may be called—

THE BLASPHEMER'S END.

In a certain town in Pennsylvania there lived a number of men who were infidels, and who had formed themselves into an infidel club. On one occasion, the members of this club met together to have a supper in the hotel. As they sat down to supper, one of their number called on the president of the club, to ask a blessing on their meal. Of course this was only done in mockery. The president complied with their request, in a way so horribly blasphemous, that it made them all roar with laughter. After this, one of the members noticed that there were just thirteen persons present. "This," he observed, " was the number reported to have been present, when Christ was said to have instituted what is called "the Lord's Supper;" and now I move, that our president take the place of Christ, and that he consecrate our supper in the same way." The president undertook to do this awfully wicked thing. He took a piece of bread and broke it, and pretended to be consecrating it, in the use of language so terribly profane, that it actually frightened some of those who were present. While doing this he suddenly stopped, turned pale, sat down in his chair, put his hand to his head, and complained of great pain. He was carried home, and put to bed. He suffered fearfully through the night, and died before the next morning dawned. Here was an instance of sin being found out, in the very act of committing it. This was awful.

But there are different ways in which sin is found out in this life. Here is a story which shows us—

HOW A LAZY BOY'S SIN FOUND HIM OUT.

Harry Smith was a little boy about ten years old. His great sin was laziness. When he was asked to do anything he would always say,— "O, it's too much trouble;" and then would give it up. One day he was sitting under a large tree, with his sister Sue, who was a very active and industrious girl, when he said,— "How I wish I had a kite, like Johnny Clarke's!"

" Well, why don't you go to work and make one, this afternoon ?" said his sister.

" Oh, it's too much trouble," said Harry, and then he stretched himself out on the grass, and went to sleep.

After tea that evening, the children gathered round the table, in the sitting-room.

" Now, for our arithmetic lesson," said Sue; " we have a long example in practical payments to work out. Come Harry, let's begin."

" I'm not going to do it," said Harry, " it's too much trouble," and he stretched himself out in the rocking-chair, where he was sitting.

Just then, their neighbor, Mr. Simpson, who

kept the apothecary's store, at the corner of the street, stepped in and said, "I haven't but a moment to spare, but I want to say, that if Harry will take hold and study Latin this winter, I'll give him a nice place in my store next spring;" and then he went out.

As soon as he was gone, Sue cried out, "O, Harry! that's splendid. Of course you'll do it."

"Not I," said Harry, "it's too much trouble," and he went on rocking in his chair.

Now let us see how Harry's sin found him out. Fifty years have gone by, since the time of which we have been speaking. Old age has overtaken him. His brothers and sisters are all well off. They are living in comfortable homes of their own. But Harry has had to go to the Alms House. There he is spending the evening of his days, in poverty and want, entirely destitute of all the comforts and enjoyments which might have been his, if he had not given way to the sin of idleness.

Harry's sin found him out in the Alms House. Our last story may be called—

MURDERERS FOUND OUT BY THE BIRDS.

The incident, of which I am now about to

speak occurred in Germany, in the year 1804, and in connection with a town called Lennep. In this town, was the only post-office, for a district of country lying around it, which embraced a number of miles.

There was a man who acted as postman for this district, whose name was Heinrich Lutz. He used to go out from Lennep, three times a week, and carry the mail, to all the villages and settlements round about the town, for several miles in different directions. He was a good and faithful man. He had been engaged in this work for a number of years, and was very much respected and loved, by all who knew him. The road over which he had to travel for some distance, lay through a deep forest, where sometimes robberies, and even murders, had been committed.

One day, in the fall of the year spoken of above, Heinrich set out as usual to go through his district, delivering the mail, which he took with him, and bringing back the letters and papers which were given him, to take to the post-office. He generally left after an early breakfast, and returned by the close of the afternoon.

In the course of his journey, on the day of

THE WARNING AGAINST SIN. 159

which we are speaking, as he was passing by the deep forest, two robbers rushed out upon him. They knocked him down, and began to beat him with their heavy clubs. While they were doing this, he said to his murderers:—" Don't think you will escape. Your sin will find you out. God can make the very birds of the air tell of you,"—pointing, as he said this, to a flock of wild birds, that were then flying over them.

The friends of Heinrich looked for his return, in Lennep that evening, but he did not come. By the next morning the sad tidings of his murder were received, and his dead body was brought home. There was a great excitement in the town all that day.

Towards the close of the afternoon, two straners came to the inn, in the town, and asked for lodging for the night, and for some supper. The wife of the keeper of the inn, waited on the strangers. Among other things, she placed a couple of roasted wild birds on the table, for them to eat. While one of the men was cutting up the birds, she heard him say to his companion:—"These birds wont tell about it, any how." This excited her surprise. As she looked carefully at the other man, she noticed some spots of blood, on his blue jacket. This alarmed her. She went at once to her husband, and told him what she had seen and heard. A constable was sent for. The men were taken up, and put in prison. On being examined the contents of the mail bag were found about their persons. Then they confessed their crime, and told what Heinrich had said about the birds, before his death.

They were tried, condemned, and hung. Their sin was found out, by means of the little birds.

But sometimes sins are not found out in this life. What then? Will the warning of our text fail, in their case? No; but they will go on to the day of judgment, and then—every sin will be found out.

Every sin that is committed is written down in the book of God's remembrance.

If we repent of our sins, the blood of Jesus will blot them all out. But, if we do not repent, they will remain written there. At the day of judgment that book will be brought forth, and then we may be sure that our sins will find us out.

And now let us look back over our sermon.

Where is our text? Numbers xxxii. 23.

What are the words of the text?—" Be sure your sin will find you out."

What is our sermon about? The warning against sin, because it is sure to be found out.

How many things did we speak of which help to make it sure? *Three.*

What is the first? *The presence of God.*

What is the second? *The power of God.*

What is the third? *The purpose of God.*

Let us all pray God to help us remember this warning, and to give us His grace that we may be kept from sinning against Him. Then we shall be able to glorify God, and our lives will be happy and useful.

" Be sure your sin will find you out."

VII.

THE WARNING AGAINST ANGER.

" Let not the sun go down upon your wrath."
                              EPHESIANS iv. 26.

THE time of the going down of the sun is generally a quiet and pleasing time. Then the labors of the day are over. Then the workman returns to his home. The birds retire to their nests. If it has been stormy during the day, the winds generally die away, and all is calm and still, when the time comes for the sun to sink below the western horizon. And if we walk out in the field, to meditate at evening time, as Isaac did, every thing around will seem to speak to us of quietness and peace. And the words of our text seem to come in very nicely, at that quiet hour when God says to us—" Let not the sun go down upon your wrath." Wrath means anger. And our sermon to-day will be about *the warning against* anger. We ought to mind this warning against anger, because if we give way to angry feelings, it will have a bad effect upon us in *three* ways.

In the first place if we give way to anger, it WILL INTERFERE WITH OUR COMFORT.

An angry man can never feel comfortable. Anger in our hearts, or minds, is just like a storm at sea. That storm, while it lasts, disturbs every thing. The waters rise and swell, and dash about in foam and fury. Any one who has ever been to sea, knows what the effect of a storm is there. As long as that storm continues it interferes, most seriously, with the comfort of all on board the vessel, which is exposed to it. The poor sailors have to face the winds and the waves, and there is no happiness for them. Most of the passengers will be made sea-sick, and be obliged to go to bed, and their comfort will be wonderfully interfered with, while that storm lasts.

And just as a storm at sea, acts on a vessel that is exposed to it, so anger acts on the soul, where its influence is felt. It upsets and disturbs all our thoughts and feelings, and interferes entirely with our comfort. Here are some practical illustrations of the way in which anger interferes with our comfort, and of the good which follows when anger is put away. Our first illustration may be called—

RETURNING GOOD FOR EVIL.

"I'll pay him back again, see if I don't," cried Tommy Smith, as he came running into the house with a flushed and angry face.

"And who are you going to pay back?" asked his mother.

"Why, Walter Jones. He took my marbles, and ran away with them. The mean chap!" said Tommy, very angrily.

"Well, I hope you will pay him back in a good way," said his mother.

Tommy hung down his head, and said nothing, for he felt ashamed to tell just what he had made up his mind to do to Walter.

"I am afraid you are going to do to Walter, something just as bad as what he has done to you. Think better of it, my son," said his mother, "and try to return good for evil. If you don't forgive you can't ask to be forgiven. And then you must feel very unhappy."

That night, before going to bed, Tommy kneeled down as usual beside his mother to say his prayers. He was nearly through and was finishing with the Lord's prayer. When he came to the place where it says, "Forgive us our trespasses as we forgive those who trespass against us," he stopped.

"Why don't you go on?" asked his mother.

"I can't," said Tommy, "because I haven't forgiven Walter Jones."

Now here we see, how Tommy's anger was interfering with his happiness. He never could be happy again unless he could say the Lord's prayer, as he had been accustomed to do.

"Then, my dear boy," said his mother, "you had better ask Jesus to help you to forgive him now."

Tommy did so, and then, feeling that his anger was gone, and that he had really forgiven Walter, he finished his prayers and went to bed feeling very happy.

Our next story may be called—

THE MINISTER'S TEMPER.

This story shows us how even a good man, may let a bad temper get the mastery over him, so as to make himself, and those about him, very uncomfortable. One day, the minister, of whom we are now speaking, was dressing himself, so as to go out and spend the afternoon in making calls among his people. But when he came to fix the collar round his neck, he found that the button was gone from his shirt, and he could not fasten the collar. All at once the good man's patience left him. He began to fret and scold, and use unkind and angry words about it, so that his poor tired wife felt very much hurt, and bursting into tears, she hastened to her own room, and sat down and had a good cry.

The minister got through with his dressing, and then went out to make his calls. He called on an old Mr. Jones, a member of his church, who was suffering greatly from rheumatism, and was unable to use his limbs. But he found him patient, and even cheerful. Then he called on a young man by the name of Hall. He was wasting away with consumption, and expecting soon to die. But he had a good hope in Jesus as his Saviour. This took away the fear of death, and made him very happy. Then he called on old grandmother Smith. She lived all by herself, in a poor miserable garret. As he was going up the stairs to her room, he heard her cheerful voice singing that sweet hymn about heaven, which begins thus—

> " There is a land of pure delight,
> Where saints immortal reign ;
> Eternal day excludes the night,
> And pleasures banish pain."

Of course he had a very pleasant visit to that good old Christian. And then the last call he made was on young Mrs. Brown. A short time before she had lost her only child, the darling of her heart. He naturally expected to find her very gloomy and sad. But to his surprise she was calm and cheerful. She said the grace of God had been sufficient to sustain her, under that heavy burden, and she felt comforted in the thought that God would make it work for good.

The minister went home at the close of that afternoon, feeling very thankful, for all that he had seen and heard. In the evening he was sitting in his easy chair before the fire, and his wife sat near him, busy with her needle. In thinking of the visits he had made to those different homes of affliction, he could not help saying—"What a wonderful thing the grace of God is! How much it can do! Nothing is too hard for it. Wonderful! wonderful! It can do all things."

"Yes, it is wonderful indeed," said his little wife; "and yet, there is *one thing*, which the grace of God does not seem to have power to do."

"And pray what can that be?" asked her husband.

"Why, it does not seem to have power to control a minister's temper, when he finds that his shirt button is gone."

In a moment the good minister's conscience smote him. He saw what a sin he had committed, in giving way to an angry temper, and how that anger had interfered with the happiness of his family. With his eyes full of tears he said —"Forgive me, my dear wife, for the wrong I have done. I will ask God to help me never to give way to such an angry temper again." And

THE WARNING AGAINST ANGER.   169

thus that minister learned to mind the Bible warning against anger.

I have one other short story for this part of our subject. We may call it—

HOW A BOY MINDED THIS WARNING.

Two little boys, both children of pious parents, got into a quarrel one day while playing a game of marbles. One of them was named Willie, and the other Charley. They did not get to striking each other; but they used very harsh words, and parted in great anger.

When Willie got home he went up to his own little room, and sat down by a window, looking out towards the west. He was feeling very unhappy, as he thought about the quarrel, which he and Charley had over their marbles. Presently, as he looked through the window, he saw the sun going slowly down the western sky. In a moment the words of our text came into his mind—"Let not the sun go down upon your wrath." Then he was startled. "I can't stand this," he said to himself. Then he rose, and put on his cap, and went out, for the purpose of going to Charley's and making up with him.

When he reached the house he rang the bell, and Charley opened the door, frowning and looking very cross at him. But Willie held out his hand to him and said: "Charley, the sun is going down; and you know the Bible says we must 'not let the sun go down upon our wrath.' Forgive me, Charley, for speaking cross to you, and let's make up."

This went straight to Charley's heart. The frown passed away from his face, and a smile came over it. He took hold of the outstretched hand, saying as he did so, "That's right, Willie. You forgive me, and I'll forgive you. And we'll make up and never be angry with each other again."

That was right. Those boys went to bed feeling very happy that night. But they never would have had a moment's happiness if they had not put away their anger.

The first reason why we ought to mind this Bible warning against anger is because it will interfere with our comfort.

The second reason for minding this warning against anger is, because IT WILL INTERFERE WITH OUR DUTY.

THE WARNING AGAINST ANGER.   171

Suppose I should wake up some morning, and on looking at my watch to see what time it was, should find that it had stopped, and was keeping time no longer. The mainspring is not broken. It was not run down, for I wound it up last night, before I went to bed. But still the watch has stopped. It will not keep time. I cannot tell what is the matter with it. After breakfast I take it to the watchmaker, and ask him to examine it, and find out what the trouble is. He opens the watch, and putting on one of his magnifying glasses, he looks carefully into it. Presently he lays it down, and says, "I see what the trouble is. A little grain of sand has got in among the works, some how or other, and that interferes with the working of the watch and makes it stop." Then he goes to work and removes that grain of sand, and after this is done, the watch goes on keeping time as usual.

Now our souls are like watches, in some respects. Our thoughts, and feelings, and desires are very much like the wheels, or works of a watch. While our feelings and tempers are all right, the wheels will go on, and the watch will keep good time. But, if we give way to a wrong feeling, or temper, like anger, it will be like the grain of sand in the works of the watch. It will stop them from going on, and the watch will not be able to keep time. And so, if we do not mind the warning of the text, and give way to anger, it will interfere with our duty. Here are some illustrations which show us how true this is. Our first story may be called—

THE KING AND THE BISHOP.

When George the Fourth, was King of England, he desired one day to receive the sacrament of the Lord's Supper, and he sent for the Bishop of Winchester to come and administer it to him. The messenger, who was sent on this errand, was very slow in his movements, and loitered along the way. This caused a long delay before the arrival of the Bishop, and the King got very impatient about it. When the Bishop came, he stated that he started immediately on getting the message, but that the servant had been very slow in coming to him. This made the King angry. He rang the bell, and called for the messenger. When he entered the room the King reproved him very sharply, dismissed him from his service, and told him to leave the palace at once. As soon as he was gone, the King turned to the Bishop, and said—"Now, my lord, we will go on with our service."

But the Bishop, with great mildness, and yet very firmly, said: "Please your majesty, I cannot do that. The temper just displayed is not a fit preparation for this solemn service." The King saw that he had done wrong, and made a suitable apology to the Bishop. Then he sent for his servant, asked his pardon for speaking so angrily to him, and told him, in the pleasantest possible way, that he should keep his position in the King's employ. And then the Bishop went on to administer the solemn sacrament to the King, and other members of his family.

And here we see how the anger of the King would have acted on him. It would have interfered with his duty, and his privilege, just as that grain of sand in the works of the watch interfered with its keeping time. But when his anger was put away, then it was all right.

Our next story may be called—

THE BEST REVENGE.

Basil Lee and Charley West were two boys about twelve years of age. They both went to the same school, and sat next to each other on the same bench.

One day, a gentleman named Mr. Raymond came to visit the school. He was a very kind gentleman, and took a great interest in the boys. After looking round the school for awhile, he went back to the teacher's desk, and said he had a sum, which he wished them to do, and that the boy who got through with it first, and did it right, should have half a dollar as a prize. A dozen or so of the larger boys began at once to try and work out this sum. Among these were Basil Lee and Charley West. Basil was very good at arithmetic. He worked away earnestly at the sum. Charley West, who sat next to him, never could do much at figures. He watched Basil slyly as he went on with his work, and as he saw the different lines of figures which he wrote down on his slate, Charley copied them on his own slate. Basil had only one more figure to put down, to finish the sum. Just then somebody went out of the school-room. Basil turned away his head, to see who it was; and while his head was turned, Charley West wet his fingers, and rubbed out the figures on Basil's slate. Then he finished the sum, and took it up to Mr. Raymond. This was the first sum finished. It was rightly done, and he got the prize of half a dollar.

Of course this made Basil very angry. As we think of it we can't help pitying him, and at the same time feeling a sort of contempt for Charley, who could do so mean and unjust a thing as that.

Just after this school was dismissed, Basil went home, feeling very much excited. On arriving there, he entered the room where his elder sister Alice was sitting sewing. As soon as he saw her he said—"I'll never forgive him as long as I live. To think of his doing so mean a thing as that! No, I'll never forgive him."

"What's the matter?" asked his sister, "and who has offended you?"

"Why, Charley West," replied Basil, as he put away his books.

"And what has Charley done to offend you? Come and sit down here by my side, and tell me all about it."

Then Basil sat down by his sister's side, and told her the story, as we have given it above. And when he got through, he said, "Now wasn't it provoking, sister? But, never mind; I'm going to have a glorious revenge on him."

"Well, my dear, and what is your revenge to be?"

"Oh, I know; and I'll tell you; for it will be just what he deserves. You see, Mr. Matthews, our teacher, has said that he will turn any boy out of school who uses the key to the Grammar Exercises. Now I saw Charley using one yesterday. So you see it is only necessary for me to tell the teacher about it. Then Charley will be dismissed from the school in disgrace. That will be my revenge; and I'm going to do this to-morrow."

"Basil, my dear," said Alice, "just listen to me for a moment. Charley has only to be at school for another year. Then, if he does well, a gentleman has offered him a situation, where he will soon be able to earn money enough to support his poor old sick mother. Of course the gentleman would not take him if he was turned out of school in disgrace. And the thought of this would break his mother's heart, and bring down her gray hairs with sorrow to the grave. Basil, are you ready for this?"

"Oh, Alice!" said Basil, "I never thought of all that; no, I wouldn't do that for the world. But I would like to punish Charley a little for his meanness."

"Well, there is a good scriptural rule, which says: 'Be not overcome of evil, but *overcome evil with good.*' Suppose you think that over, and see what you can do."

Basil did so; and the end of it was, that a day or two after, he sent Charley an invitation, to come the next Saturday, and spend the afternoon, and take tea with him. Charley was greatly surprised to get this invitation; but he accepted it and went. They had a pleasant afternoon, though Charley couldn't help feeling ashamed of himself when he thought how meanly he had treated Basil.

In the large garden of Basil's father, was a beautiful pond of water. The boys spent their time in sailing a number of little boats, which Basil had made, on the pond. The largest of those boats Basil called—the Hero. Charley was particularly pleased with this. And when he was going home, after tea, Basil made him a present of the boat he had liked so much. This was too much for Charley. His eyes filled with tears, as he looked at Basil, and said, "My dear fellow! I can't tell you how ashamed of myself I feel, for the mean way in which I treated you. I need not ask you to forgive me, for your conduct shows that you have done that. You have overcome my evil with your goodness. I shall never forget your kindness as long as I live. And it will keep me forever from doing so mean a thing again."

Now suppose that Basil had let the sun go down upon his wrath, and had kept alive his anger towards Charley, we see how it would have interfered with his usefulness and duty.

Like the grain of sand in the works of the watch, it would have stopped it from keeping time.

The second reason for minding this warning

against anger is, that it will interfere with our duty.

And the third reason for minding this warning against anger is, that it will—INTERFERE WITH OUR SAFETY.

In old times, before the invention of gunpowder, and the use of firearms, the safety of a soldier, depended chiefly on the armor which he had about his limbs and body, and the shield which he carried before him. There would be no safety in these now, when cannon balls, and rifle bullets are the chief weapons of war. But when swords, and spears, and bows and arrows were what men fought with, it was very different. Then a soldier could go into battle with safety, if he had his armor on, and carried his shield before him. Anything that deprived him of these, would interfere with his safety.

And it is just so with ourselves, in the warfare of life in which we are engaged. Here, we too, need a shield and armor. And there can be no safety for us, unless we have these. The apostle Paul tells us about "a shield of faith," and "a breastplate and armor of righteousness," which we must have if we hope to be safe in doing our duty. These refer to the protection against sin, and Satan, which God affords to all his people. He said to Abraham, "Fear not; I am thy shield." And when Satan tried to injure Job, he found that he could not get near him, or hurt a hair of his head. And the reason was, he was obliged to confess, that "God had put a hedge about him, and about all that he had," so that no one could hurt him. And what was true of Job, is true of all God's people. He is their shield, their hedge, their armor, their defence, and safeguard.

But if we commit sin; if we do what we know is wrong; if we let the sun go down upon our wrath, and give way to anger, then, we are doing that which will interfere with our safety. Our shield and armor will be taken away, and we shall be exposed to all sorts of dangers.

Here are some illustrations of this part of our subject. Our first story may be called—

MAKING UP WITH GOD.

A little boy came to his father one day and said—

"O papa, I have made up with God."

"Why, my dear boy, what do you mean? I hope you had not fallen out with God, had you?"

"Yes, papa, I had. I got angry with Charley Jones, when we were playing marbles, and I spoke very crossly to him, and called him bad names. After we had parted, and I came to think it all over, I could not help feeling very unhappy. I knew that God was angry with me. And then I was sure I never could have any comfort, and never feel that I was safe. So I went to my room and told God about my sin. With bitter tears I asked him to forgive my sin, and not to feel angry with me for what I had done. I know that God heard my prayer. And now I feel happy, because I am sure that I am safe."

What a beautiful example this dear child sets us! He was minding the Bible warning against anger, because he felt sure it would interfere with his safety.

Our next story may be called—

THE SAD RESULT OF ANGER.

Two boys, whose names were Robert and Frank, were playing together with their top. They only had one top between them. First one of them would spin it, and then the other. They got on together very well for some time. But after awhile they got to quarrelling about it. Frank said — "It's my turn to spin the top now." "No, it's not. It's my turn," said Robert. "You lie," said Frank, as he doubled up his fist, and hit him a heavy blow. Then they both got very angry, and began to fight. Robert was getting the better of the fight, when Frank took a big sharp knife from his pocket, and plunged it into his companion's heart. He fell to the ground, and died in a few moments. How sad this was! Here we see the terrible effects of anger. If those two boys had only learned to mind the Bible warning against this sin, how different their lives would have been! But they allowed anger to get the mastery of them, and we see how it interfered with their safety! One of them lost his life, and his soul too; for dying as he did, in the very act of sinning against God, of course he could not go to heaven; and the other lost his character. He was a murderer,—and as such he was sent to prison for years.

How careful we should be to mind this warning against anger!

I have just one more short story before closing. We may call it—

THE EFFECT OF ANGER UPON US.

A young man called on the minister, to whose church he belonged, one day, to talk with him about a matter that was giving him a good deal of trouble. "My friend James Johnson, has acted very meanly towards me several times lately," said the young man. "This has made me very angry, and now I've determined to have my revenge."

The minister talked with him very faithfully about it. He tried to show him that this was not at all a Christian spirit; that he ought to overcome his anger, and leave it with God to settle the matter, as "vengeance belongeth unto Him." But the young man said, "No, I am going to have my revenge." "Well, my young friend, let us kneel down together, and pray over it, before you go on any further in the matter."

Then the minister began to pray, in this way—

"O Lord, it will not be necessary that Thou shouldest defend this young man any longer. He is going to seek his own revenge, and he feels that he is able to take care of himself, and provide for his own safety." "Please stop," said the young man. "I never thought of that; of course I am not prepared for that." Then he finished the prayer which the minister had begun, by saying, "O God, forgive my great sin in this matter. Help me to overcome my anger, and leave revenge with Thee, for Jesus' sake. Amen."

Now, where is our text to-day? Ephesians iv. 26. What are the words of the text? "Let not the sun go down upon your wrath." What is the sermon about? The Bible warning against anger. We ought to mind this warning for how many reasons? *Three.* In the first place, if we give way to anger, it will interfere with what? With our *comfort.* In the second place, with what? With our *duty*. And in the third place, with what? With our *safety*. Then let us pray that we may have "the same mind that was also in Christ Jesus," and be able by the grace of God to—"tread in the blessed steps of his most holy life." Then all angry feelings will be subdued within us, and we shall

"LET NOT THE SUN GO DOWN UPON OUR WRATH."

VIII.

THE WARNING AGAINST GRIEVING THE SPIRIT.

"*Grieve not the Holy Spirit of God.*"
EPHESIANS iv. 30.

THE Spirit of God is given to us to be our teacher, and helper, in trying to love and serve God. We please this blessed Spirit when we listen to his gentle whispers, and try to carry them out. We grieve this Holy Spirit when we do not mind His teachings, and try to do the things which He wants us to do.

Now one of the greatest blessings that God ever can bestow upon us, is the gift of the Holy Spirit. We know what a great blessing the heart is in our body, because if the heart were not here beating, beating, all the time, there would be no circulation of the blood; and then we could not live. We know what a blessing the eyes are to our heads, because without them we should be blind, and never able to see anything. We know what a blessing the mainspring is to a watch, because without it the works could not go on, and the watch would not keep time. We know what a blessing steam is to a locomotive engine, when it is finished, and ready for work ; because without steam, it can do nothing, and never be of any use. There is a captain going to sea in a new vessel. What a blessing to that ship it is to have a good rudder, fastened to her stern, because without a rudder the vessel cannot be steered ; and so, before long, it will either be run ashore, or dashed against the rocks, and be broken to pieces.

And these different cases all help to show what a blessing the Holy Ghost is to us. For just what the heart is to the body ; what the eyes are to the head ; what the main-spring is to the watch ; what the steam is to the locomotive ; or what the rudder is to the ship, *just this*, and *more*, the Holy Spirit is to us, in trying to get to heaven.

And here, in our text, we have *the Bible warning against grieving the Holy Spirit This*, is the subject of our present sermon. And I wish to speak of four reasons, why we ought to mind this warning. And these reasons refer to the different ways, in which it will injure us, if we do grieve the Spirit. *And in the first place, we ought to mind this warning, because grieving the Spirit will*—INJURE OUR KNOWLEDGE.

Of ourselves, we have no knowledge of the way to heaven, and never could tell how to get there. It is the Holy Spirit alone, who can give us this knowledge. But if we grieve the Spirit, we shall never get this knowledge.

Suppose that you and I, were travelling through a strange country, like Switzerland. We should have no knowledge of the right way to travel in, so as to get safely through the country. And this would make it necessary for us to have a guide to show us the way. I remember when the Rev. Dr. Cooper of this city, and myself, were travelling through Switzerland, some years ago, an incident occurred, which may come in as a good illustration of this part of our subject. We were stopping at an inn, in the beautiful valley of Interlachen, and had made arrangements, one evening, to go on

foot the next day, over a high mountain called "the Wengern Alp," to the valley of Lauterbrunnen, on the other side. We had engaged a guide to show us the way, and were to take an early start the next morning. There was an English traveller, staying at the same inn with us. He was travelling alone, and wanted to take the same journey. He spoke to one of the guides about going with him. But he thought the man asked too much money. They could not agree about the price ; so he refused to take the guide, and said he was sure he could find the way himself. He started, all by himself, the next morning, a good while before us. When we had gotten nearly half way over the mountain our guide stopped. He pointed to a dark looking little object, far off from the path in which we were walking, and said :

"There's the gentleman who would not have a guide. He has lost his way. He never can get out of the mountains in that direction. If he doesn't come back, he'll lose his life." Then the guide climbed up on a high piece of ground, and putting his hands to his mouth, he called out as loudly as he could, "Come back!"

come back!" We could not tell whether the lost man heard him or not, or what became of him. But in refusing to take a guide to show him the way, that man was injuring his knowledge, just as we do, when we grieve the Holy Spirit.

Here is a story which comes in very well to illustrate this point. We may call it—

HOW ALICE FOUND THE WAY TO HEAVEN.

Alice was a young girl, about fourteen years of age. Her parents were very rich, and she was their only child. But she was taken sick. When the doctor came and examined her case, he said the disease was one which could not be cured, and that she had but a short time to live. Then she became anxious about her soul. Her parents were not Christians, and knew very little about religion. "Father," she said one day, "the doctor says I have not long to live. When I die, where shall I go?"

But her father could not answer the question.

"Mother dear, can you not tell me what I must do to get to heaven?"

But her mother had nothing to say.

"Father," she exclaimed again, "is there no one who can tell me what I must do to be saved?"

"My child," said her father, "you have always been a good girl—a dutiful daughter. You have never grieved your parents. You have regularly attended church, and taken part in its services. Don't you think that is all you need?"

"Oh! no, my dear father. That will not do. I cannot rest my soul there. That is not the way to heaven. Oh! I am going to die. I know not what will become of me. Can no one show me the way to heaven?"

Now Alice had a young girl to wait on her. She was a member of the church and an earnest Christian. She asked permission to go and bring her minister to answer these great questions. She was told to go. The minister came, and sat down by the bedside of the dying girl. She raised herself on her elbow, and looking earnestly at him, said—

"Sir, can you tell me what I must *do* to find rest for my soul, and to die at peace with God?"

"No, my friend," said the minister, "I cannot tell what—*you can do*, but I can tell you, what *has been done for you.*" And then he told her about the sufferings and death of Jesus. "He did all this," said the minister, "to obtain pardon and salvation for poor sinners, such as we are. And now, this one short verse shows us the way to heaven—" Believe on the Lord Jesus Christ, and thou shalt be saved."

"Yes, I believe that Jesus died for sinners," said Alice, "but how can I be sure that He died *for me?*"

"You may be sure of that, my young friend," said the minister, "from what he said Himself, when He was on earth. These are His own sweet words. Listen to them: 'God so loved the world, that He gave His only begotten Son, that *whosoever*'—this takes in you, and me, and everybody—'that *whosoever* believeth in Him should not perish, but have everlasting life.'"

"I see it now, sir; thank you, thank you, a thousand times!" said Alice. "And now, sir, won't you please to kneel down and pray that my sins may be pardoned, and my soul may be saved for Jesus' sake?"

He kneeled down with all the family, and offered an earnest prayer in her behalf.

When the prayer was ended, she said, "Now,

I feel perfectly willing to die, whenever the time shall come." Not many days after, the time did come, and she died a peaceful and happy death.

Now when this young girl found out that she was going to die, it was the Spirit of God who put into her heart the desire to find out the way of salvation. And it was listening to His voice, which secured to her a knowledge of that way. If she had refused to listen to the Spirit's voice, then she would have been grieving the Spirit, and that would have injured her knowledge. She never would have found out the way of salvation, or have known how to get to heaven. And so, the first reason why we ought to mind this warning, and not grieve the Spirit, is because it will injure our knowledge.

The second reason why we ought to mind this warning, is because grieving the Spirit—WILL INJURE OUR HAPPINESS.

When David was speaking of the happy effect, which follows from our acquaintance with the truth of God, he said—"Blessed are the people which know the joyful sound." This blessedness refers to the happiness which God's people find from knowing Him. And here we see how the knowledge of God, and the happiness which springs from it, both go together. This knowledge is like a fountain; and this happiness is like the stream which flows from the fountain. But we cannot have the stream, unless we have the fountain too. And so we see, that if grieving the Spirit interferes with our knowledge of God, it must, in just the same way, interfere with the happiness which springs from that knowledge. Now let us look at some incidents, which illustrate this part of our subject, and show us how true it is, that if we do not grieve the Spirit, but listen to His teachings, we shall find the knowledge of salvation, and this knowledge will be sure to make us happy.

Our first illustration is from the New Testament. In the eighth chapter of the Acts of the Apostles, we read about an Ethiopian Eunuch. He was a great man under Candace, the Queen of the Ethiopians, and had charge of all her treasures. He lived far down in Africa, a long, long distance from Jerusalem. But he was a pious Jew, and had travelled all the way to Jerusalem, to attend the great feast of the Passover. While he was there, he had heard the wonderful story of Jesus ; how He had been put to death on the cross ;—had been buried ;—had risen from the dead, and ascended into heaven. This was all very strange to him, and he could not understand it. But he was very anxious to know more about it. He could not wait till he reached home, to try and find out the meaning of it. He had with him that part of the Old Testament which contained the prophets, and so as he sat riding along in his chariot, he was reading aloud.

Now it happened, in the providence of God, that just then, Philip the Evangelist, was going through that part of the country, preaching the gospel. As he saw this chariot coming along, the Spirit of God told him to go up to the chariot. He did so. As he came near, he heard the Ethiopian reading the Bible aloud, and asked him, if he understood what he was reading? He said he did not, and asked Philip to come and sit by him and help him. Philip sat down by his side. He found that he was reading that part of the fifty-third chapter of Isaiah, where it says—" he was led as a lamb to the slaughter," etc. The Ethiopian asked—whether the prophet was speaking of himself there, or of some one else. And then we are told that "Philip began at the same scripture, and preached unto him Jesus." We have no report given of what he said to the Ethiopian. No doubt he told him that the prophet was speaking there of Jesus, the Saviour of the world. Then I suppose, he went on to tell him how Jesus had come into the world: How he had died upon the cross for our sins;—how he was buried, and rose again on the third day, and had ascended into heaven;—and how, before His ascension, He had sent forth his servants through all the world, to preach the gospel;—and that all who wished to be saved by Him, must be baptized in His name, and confess themselves His friends and followers. As he was saying this, they passed by a stream of water. The Ethiopian pointed to it, and said: "See, here is water; what doth hinder me to be baptized?" Philip answered, "if thou believest with all thy heart, thou mayest." And he said, "I believe that Jesus Christ is the Son of God." Then Philip baptized him, and we read "that he went on his way rejoicing."

Now here we see how eager this Ethiopian was, to know about Jesus, and the way to heaven. And we see, too, how earnestly he listened to the voice of the Spirit, speaking through his servant Philip. By doing this, he found the knowledge of God, and that made him happy. But if he had grieved the Holy Spirit, by refusing to listen to his voice, he never would have got the knowledge of the way to heaven, and never would have felt the happiness of those who walk in it. Grieving the Spirit would have injured both his knowledge and his happiness. Our next illustration may be called—

NOW I SEE IT, OR THE RUSSIAN SERVANT GIRL'S EXPERIENCE.

This story is told by an English clergyman, who lived in St. Petersburg, a number of years, having the charge of an English chapel there.

"We had several Russian servants," he says, "among whom was a bright intelligent young woman, whose name was Erena. She came to us in the fall of the year, and everything went on well, till the beginning of Lent, in the spring of the following year. Erene was a member of the Greek Church. The persons belonging to this Church are very particular in keeping the fast of Lent, and attend the services of this season, as diligently as though their salvation depended on it. Erene told her mistress, that she wished to attend Church twice every day, all through Lent. Her mistress told her that she ought not to think of going so often."

"Do you wish me to lose my soul, ma'am?" asked the girl. "No," was the answer,—"far from it: I wish your soul to be saved. But fasting, and saying prayers, and going to church will not save your soul. There must be something more than all this. The Lord Jesus Christ is the only Saviour of sinners, and it is *by faith in Him alone*, that any can be saved."

"Ah," said Erena, "that is your religion; but I have been taught differently, and I must follow my own religion."

Erena's mistress had taught her to read, and had given her a Russian Testament.

"One Sunday, when we were going to Chapel," says this good minister, "my wife left Erena in charge of the children. Before leaving, she asked Erena to please read the tenth chapter of the Acts of the Apostles, while we were away. This excited her curiosity. She wondered what there could be in that chapter, which made her mistress so anxious for her to read it. She began to read it at once, and got very much interested in the account given there, of Cornelius the centurion. When she read about his fasting, and praying, and giving alms, she was very much interested, and said:—" Ah! this is delightful! This man was of my religion. He believed in fasting, praying, and giving alms." But when she found that an angel was sent to him, to show him how he could get to "*hear words whereby he might be saved,*" she could not understand what this meant. As soon as we returned from church, she came to my wife with great earnestness, and said—" Please ma'am, will you explain this to me? I can't understand it. Here is a good man, who kept the fast, and prayed to God, and gave alms; but that was not enough. Now why was it not enough? I never was taught to do anything more."

"Well, Erena," said her mistress, "just read the chapter carefully through, and you will find out why the angel was sent to Cornelius."

Then she went to her room, and read carefully on, till she came to that beautiful verse, where Peter says of Christ,—"To Him give all the prophets witness, that through His name, *whosoever believeth in Him* shall receive remission of sins." This was enough. For the first time in her life, she clearly saw how, we are to be saved through Jesus. She had found out the way to heaven. Running to her mistress, she clasped her hands, and exclaimed—

"O ma'am! I see it now—I see it now—I see it now! It was not by fasting, that Cornelius the centurion was to be saved; it was not by saying prayers—it was not by giving alms—but it was by believing on *Jesus the Son of God*. I never saw it before, but I see it now."

That Russian servant had found out the way to heaven. She began to walk in it at once, and it made her happy. But if she had refused to read the Testament that her mistress gave her, she would have been grieving the Spirit. That would have injured both her knowledge, and her happiness.

And here we see that the second reason why

we should mind this warning, is—because grieving the Spirit will injure our happiness.

The third reason why we should mind this warning, is because—GRIEVING THE SPIRIT WILL INJURE OUR USEFULNESS.

If you are an errand boy in a store, and your duty is to carry parcels, or messages, wherever you are sent, then if anything should make you lame, so that you could not walk,—*this* would interfere with your usefulness. Suppose you have a position on one of the stations of the Pennsylvania Railway. Your duty there, is to watch the signals, which tell when a train is coming; and then to give notice of it, by ringing a bell. And suppose that something should happen to your eyes, so that you could not see; this would at once injure your usefulness, and unfit you for the duties of your position.

Or suppose, that your mother is a very skilful seamstress, and is supporting her family by the diligent use of her needle. She has an attack of rheumatism, which settles on her right hand, making her fingers so stiff, that she cannot use her needle. That would injure her usefulness.

And it is just so with us, in trying to serve

God. If we listen to the voice of the Spirit, when he speaks to us, and mind what he says, then he will show us what our duty is, and help us to do it. And that will make us useful. But if we grieve the Spirit, by not listening to His voice, then we shall never know what our duty is, and we should have no power to do it, even if we did know.

We have a good illustration of this part of our subject, in the case of Judas Iscariot. He was one of the twelve apostles, chosen by our Saviour. He was with him all through the years of His public ministry. He saw the miracles he performed, and heard His teachings, both in public and in private. And yet, at last, he basely betrayed his Master for thirty pieces of silver. Now suppose, that instead of listening to Satan, when he came and tempted him to commit that horrible sin, he had resisted that temptation, and had been faithful to his Master; then, like Peter and John, he would have spent the rest of his life, in preaching the glorious gospel, and would have been a blessing to multitudes of souls. But instead of this, he yielded to Satan's temptation, and grieved the Spirit by betraying his Master.

And how that injured his usefulness, we see when we think, that instead of being made the means of saving souls from death, it led him to go and hang himself!

I have one other illustration for this part of our subject. We may call it—

SORELY TEMPTED.

It shows us how a boy was kept from injuring his usefulness, by not grieving the Spirit, but by listening to his voice. This boy's name was Tommy Wright. He was about fifteen years old, and the only son of his mother, who was very fond of him.

Mrs. Wright had got a situation for him in a merchant's store. When he was about leaving home, to begin work in this new place, his mother said to him : "Now Tommy, before you go, there are two promises I want you to make me."

"What are they, mother?" he asked, looking fondly into her loving face, which was always so calm and peaceful.

"Promise me first, that you will always, wherever you are, no matter how busy, read one or more verses in the Bible every day; and then promise me next, that you will never take a penny that is not your own."

"The first is easy enough, mother dear," said Tommy; "but I don't like the second at all. It seems almost like an insult. You know very well I have not been brought up to be a thief. Surely you don't imagine, for a moment, that I would ever steal?"

"Give me the promise, Tommy dear," said his mother, "and I will pray for you, as you must pray for yourself, that God will give you grace to keep your word. These are terrible times, that we are living in. Men who stand high in honor, are often known to do very mean, and dishonorable things. The fairest reputations are blighted. The city is full of snares, and I don't know what temptations you may meet with. You will need God's help every day, to keep you from doing wrong."

So Tommy made the promise, and then his mother kneeled down with him, and in her simple earnest words, asked the Lord to go with her dear boy, and help him to do his duty, in the new position he was about to occupy,

WARNING AGAINST GRIEVING THE SPIRIT.

and to keep him from ever doing what was wrong.

For some time, after entering on the duties of his new position, Tommy got on very well. He read every day at least one verse from the Bible. Sometimes he would read a number of verses, and occasionally a whole chapter. But after a while, he began to be careless about it. Occasionally he would omit his reading in the morning, intending to do it at night, and at night deferring it till the next day. Then he would forget to pray. The next wrong step was his going with bad companions.

His anxious, loving mother, up at the old farm, felt sure that he was not doing well, for his letters were few and short. But she kept on praying for him with increasing earnestness.

At last he got into debt, and was at a loss to know what to do. One day he was left alone, at the close of the day, in a room where there was an unlocked drawer, with a large sum of money in it, in notes and silver. Just then Satan came and tempted him. He said to him, "Why can't you take some of this money, and get out of debt? Mr. Courtnay, your employer, will never find it out. And when you get your wages, if you like, you can pay it back."

Tommy made up his mind to do this. He went to the drawer, and took a handful of silver; but just as he was about to put it into his coat-pocket, he was startled by what seemed like some one whispering in his ear. The quiet voice seemed to say: "Tommy Wright! Tommy Wright! Take care! Remember the promise you made to your mother."

In a moment, he put the money back in the drawer, and went home. On arriving there, he went straight up to his little room, and kneeling down, in great distress, and with many tears, he confessed his sin to God, and asked to be forgiven. Then he prayed that God would help him to resist every such temptation in the future, and always do what was right.

Now it was the Spirit of God, who whispered those warning words in Tommy's ear. He listened to the Spirit's voice, and that kept him from doing wrong. But if he had not minded those whispered words, he would have grieved the Spirit. And then he would have gone on from one sin to another, till he lost his situation, and so he would have injured his usefulness. And here we see, that the third reason why we should mind this warning is, because grieving the Spirit will—injure our usefulness.

The fourth reason why we should mind this warning is, because grieving the Spirit—WILL CAUSE THE LOSS OF OUR SOULS.

Just see what it says in the other part of the verse in which our text is found. "Grieve not the holy Spirit of God—*whereby ye are sealed, unto the day of redemption.*" To seal the soul unto the day of redemption, is to make its salvation sure. This is what the Spirit will do for those who listen to his voice. But if we grieve the Spirit, by refusing to listen to his voice, He will stop speaking to us, and leave us to ourselves, and then our souls will certainly be lost.

See, there is Noah's ark, just finished. God told Noah and all his family to come into the ark. They listened to His voice. They all went into the ark; and when the flood came, they were saved. But suppose now they had not minded what God said to them, and had refused to go into the ark; that would have been like grieving the Spirit; and the result would have been, that when the flood came, they would all have been destroyed. And so if we go on grieving the Spirit, it must certainly result in the loss of our souls.

Now let us look at some illustrations of the sad results which must always follow those who go on grieving the Spirit. Our first story may be called—

TIME ENOUGH YET.

One day a gentleman was stopped, as he was going along the street in New York, by a shabby-looking man, who asked him if he did not remember his old college classmate, Harry Brown? and then begged him to lend him five dollars.

The gentleman remembered Harry Brown very well. His father was a very rich man, and when they were in college, Harry's business prospects were better than those of any other member of the class. He looked with surprise on this man's dirty, thread-bare clothes, and asked, " Can it be possible, that you are my old friend and classmate, Harry Brown ?"

" It is just so," said he.

WARNING AGAINST GRIEVING THE SPIRIT.

"Well, do tell me, Harry, what has brought you to this sad condition of poverty and want?"

"'Time enough yet,' has brought me to this state," said the poor man very sadly. "I got into the way of saying this, whenever I was asked to do anything. I used always to put off doing things at the right time. This ruined my business. If I had only formed the habit of doing at once, what I knew was right to be done, I might have been a rich man now. I was once almost persuaded to be a Christian, and join the church; but I put it off with—'Time enough yet;' and since then I have never felt the slightest interest in the subject of religion. I am ruined in body, and in soul, for time, and for eternity—by this short sentence—'Time enough yet.'" This was very sad. That man had grieved the Holy Spirit, and it ended in the loss of his soul.

I have one other illustration. We may call it—

THE SAD RESULT OF GRIEVING THE SPIRIT.

This story is told by a faithful minister of the Gospel, as connected with his own experience while in college.

"We had," said he, "a remarkable revival of religion, one winter, during my college course. A large number of the students in my class, became Christians and joined the church, while that revival was going on. There was one young man in our class, who was an unusually bright student. His manners were very pleasing, and he was a great favorite with all the students. He attended the revival meetings for several weeks, and was under great exercise of mind. I was very anxious for his conversion, as I felt sure that he would make an uncommonly useful Christian. I prayed for him continually, and had many earnest conversations with him on the subject. But there seemed to be some difficulty in his way, and I felt very anxious about him. One evening he came to my room, and in the course of our conversation he said to me—"I am very much obliged to you, my friend, for the warm interest you have taken in my case, during this revival. I have come to tell you that the question is settled at last, but in a different way from what you have expected. I have made up my mind not to become a Christian, now. You see I have always intended, when I get through College, to enter into political life. But I feel sure that I never should succeed as a politician, if I were an earnest Christian. So I have concluded to make politics my choice, and let religion go."

"I was greatly distressed," said the good minister, "when I heard this. With the tears streaming down my face, I pleaded most earnestly with him, not to take this course. But all that I could say had no effect on him. He had made his choice, and was resolved to stand by it.

When his college course was finished, he entered into political life. He was successful in his efforts. He won great honor as a politician. But what was the end of it? He finally became intemperate and *went down at last, to a drunkard's grave.* And we know that God has said—"Drunkards shall not inherit the kingdom of God."

Now that young man was grieving the Holy Spirit of God, when he made up his mind not to be a Christian, at the time of that revival in his college life. He did not mind the warning of our text: and the end of it was—*the loss of his soul.*

Now where is our text to-day? Ephesians iv. 30. What are the words of the text? "Grieve not the holy Spirit of God." What is the sermon about? The warning against grieving the Spirit. How many reasons did we have for minding this warning? Four. In the first place, we ought to mind this warning because grieving the Spirit will do what? *Injure our knowledge.* In the second place, because it will do what? *Injure our happiness.* In the third place, because it will do what? *Injure our usefulness.* And in the fourth place, because it will do what? *Cause the loss of our souls.*

Now let us make up our minds, that by the help of God, we will never grieve the Spirit. And how are we to do this? Why, by always listening to the voice of the Spirit, when he speaks to us. And how may we know when the Spirit is speaking to us? Why, whenever we feel in our hearts a desire to do what is right, or not to do what is wrong,—it is the Spirit who puts that desire there. That is the way in which He speaks to us. If we listen to His voice it will be well with us; if we don't listen to his voice, then we shall be grieving the Spirit: and that will bring upon us all the evils of which we have spoken.

Here is a short prayer, made up of two collects, which closes this sermon, very suitably:

"O God, who didst teach the hearts of thy faithful people by sending to them the light of thy Holy Spirit; grant us by the same Spirit to have a right judgment in all things, that we may both perceive and know what things we ought to do, and also may have grace and power faithfully to fulfil the same; through Jesus Christ our Lord. *Amen.*"

IX.

THE WARNING AGAINST BREAKING THE SABBATH.

"*Remember the Sabbath day to keep it holy.*"
                                    EXODUS xx. 9.

THESE words are part of one of the Ten Commandments, which God gave to the Israelites at Mount Sinai. We may regard them as God's command to us to keep the Sabbath, or as His warning against breaking it. And so, our sermon to-day is about—

THE WARNING AGAINST BREAKING THE SABBATH.

And I wish to speak of *three* reasons why we ought to mind this warning.

In the first place, we ought to mind it—FOR OUR OWN SAKES.

It is God's command to us to keep the Sabbath holy. And David tells us that—"in keeping his commandments there is great reward." This brings the matter home personally, to each one of us. In Isaiah lvi. 2, God says—"Blessed is the man that keepeth the Sabbath from polluting it." And in the 5th verse of this chapter, the Lord goes on to tell how He will bless those who keep the Sabbath. He says—"Even unto them will I give in my house, and within my walls, a place and a name, better than of sons and daughters, and I will give them an everlasting name that shall not be cut off." This shows us how truly we should mind this warning for our own sakes. It will bring God's special blessing upon us, and that will do us more good than all the gold and silver in the world, without it. Now let us look at some illustrations of the blessings which come on those who keep the Sabbath. Our first illustration is—

SIR MATTHEW HALE'S EXPERIENCE ABOUT THE SABBATH.

This good man was, for many years, a judge in England. He was one of the best and wisest judges that England ever had, and he was an eminent Christian.

And this is what he said, after forty years' experience and observation about the Sabbath. "I have noticed," he said, "that whenever I undertook any worldly business on the Lord's day, that business never prospered. Nay, I have noticed that if I even planned, or thought about any temporal business on that day, it never prospered. So that I was always afraid even to think of any worldly business on the Sabbath."

"Nay, more than this," said Judge Hale, "I have noticed that the more diligent, and careful I was, in attending properly, to the duties and privileges of the Lord's day, the more happy and successful I was in my business during the following week; so that, from the way in which I kept the Sabbath, I could always tell how I might expect to prosper in the employments of the ensuing week."

The testimony of Sir Matthew Hale about the Sabbath, has been put into verse by some one, in this way—

> "A Sunday well spent
> Brings a week of content,
> And health for the toils of the morrow;
> But a Sabbath profaned,
> Whatsoe'er may be gained,
> Is a certain forerunner of sorrow."

And the experience of a great and good man, like Sir Matthew Hale, should lead us all to mind this warning about breaking the Sabbath, for our own sakes.

Our next story may be called—

THE SABBATH A BLESSING.

"A young man, who was a member of my church," said a faithful minister, "came to me one day, saying that he was in great trouble, and wanted me to advise him what to do." "What is the matter, my young friend?" I asked.

"My employer wants me to work on the Sabbath. I must either lose my place, or break the Sabbath. Now which would you advise me to do?"

Without a moment's hesitation I said: "Let your place go, and honor God's holy day. If you think my friend, that God can't open another door as quickly, and as widely, as that which your employer can shut against you, then you might hesitate. But you know He *can;* and I feel sure He will. Trust Him, and do what you know is right."

The young man took my advice. He gave up

his place, for conscience' sake, and honored God by trusting Him.

I will not stop to tell what took place immediately after this. It is more than twenty years since this occurred. But that young man now has the title of "Hon." attached to his name. He has been greatly prospered in business, and is worth more than half a million of dollars. And all this comes from God's blessing upon him for keeping the Sabbath. Surely, for *our own sakes*, we ought to mind the warning against breaking this holy day.

An infidel once said to a friend—"I have learned, by sad experience, that a curse is sure to follow those who break the Sabbath."

And here is a short story which shows the truth of that infidel's statement. We may call it—

THE DIFFERENCE BETWEEN HONORING, AND DISHONORING THE SABBATH.

At a successful boarding-house, some years ago, there were fifteen young men boarding. They were all respectable young men, engaged in business of different kinds, and all having the prospect of doing well. Six of those young men were always present at the breakfast table, on Sunday morning, shaved, and well-dressed, and ready, after breakfast, to go to church. Their custom was to go regularly to church, both in the morning, and the afternoon of the Sabbath. With the other nine young men it was very different. They never appeared at the breakfast table, on Sunday morning, but would sleep on till late in the morning, and only get up in time to be ready for dinner. After dinner they would go out, but not to church. Instead of this, they would spend the rest of the holy day, either in sailing on the river, or driving into the country, or walking through the public park.

Now notice the difference between these two sets of young men. Observe how differently they began their business life. Six of them made up their minds to honor God, by keeping His day holy. Nine of them determined to do as they pleased in this matter. They dishonored God by breaking the Sabbath day, which he had commanded should be kept holy. And what was the effect on those young men, in after life, of the different way in which they regarded God's holy day? The six young men, who honored the Sabbath, had God's blessing resting upon them. They were all prosperous in business, and became highly respected citizens.

But how different it was with the other nine! They are all dead but one, and he has always had to struggle hard for a living. The other eight all failed in business. They led wicked and useless lives. Several of them became intemperate, and went down to drunkards' graves: and two of them committed murder, and ended their lives on the gallows.

An aged clergyman in Baltimore states, that during the many years he was Chaplain to the Maryland Penitentiary, he took great pains to find out from the convicts, what was the commencement of their downward course; and the testimony of ninety-nine out of a hundred, was that the beginning of their wicked courses was, —*breaking the Sabbath.*

A distinguished merchant in New York, who had been a careful observer of the things around him, and had gained an uncommon knowledge of men, said to a friend one day: "When I see one of my clerks riding out on the Sabbath, I dismiss him on Monday morning, because I am sure that a young man who is willing to break God's law, is not to be trusted."

And these instances all show us, how true it is that we should mind this warning against breaking the Sabbath—in the first place—*for our own sake.*

In the second place, we ought to mind this warning for the sake of our country.

One reason why God appointed the Sabbath among the Israelites, was that it might prove a blessing to them, as a nation. And in the prophecy of Isaiah—(ch. lviii. 13, 14)—we find Him giving a special promise, which shows how directly the prosperity of their country was made dependent on the proper observance of the Sabbath day. In this passage, God is speaking to the Jews, as a nation, when He says: " If thou turn away thy foot from the Sabbath, from doing thy pleasure on my holy day; and call the Sabbath a delight, the holy of the Lord, honorable; and shalt honor Him, not doing thine own ways, nor finding thine own pleasure, nor speaking thine own words: then shalt thou delight thyself in the Lord; and I will cause thee to ride upon the high-places of the earth, and feed thee with the heritage of Jacob thy father: for the mouth of the Lord hath spoken it." Here we are taught that keeping the Sabbath will promote the prosperity of our country.

And then, there is another passage of scripture, which shows us just as plainly, that if we break the Sabbath, we shall bring the curse of God upon our country. When the Jews failed to keep the Sabbath, this was one of the chief causes, on account of which they were led into captivity, by the king of Babylon. After their return to Jerusalem, Nehemiah was sent by God to be their governor.

In talking to the princes of Judah one day, Nehemiah used these words: "What evil thing is this that ye do, to profane the Sabbath-day? Did not your fathers thus, and did not our God bring all this evil upon us, and upon this city? Yet ye bring more wrath upon Israel by profaning the Sabbath." Neh. xiii. 17, 18.

It was true, that with the Jews, keeping the Sabbath, brought God's blessing upon their country, and made it prosper; but breaking the

Sabbath, interfered with their prosperity, as a nation, and brought distress and trouble upon them.

And there are plenty of facts, to prove that the same thing is true in reference to ourselves. If we keep God's day holy, as He commands us to do, we shall be helping to bring a blessing on our country; but if we allow ourselves to break the Sabbath, then the country in which we live, will have to suffer for our sin. Let us look now at some illustrations of this part of our subject.

Our first illustration may be called—

THE EFFECTS OF SABBATH-BREAKING.

Some years ago, there were two neighboring villages, in the State of New Hampshire. In one of these villages, there were six families, that lived in the constant neglect of the Sabbath. In the other, there were five families, who were careful to keep this day holy, as God has commanded us to do. Now, let us follow the history of these two sets of families, and notice what effect their treatment of the Sabbath had upon them.

Look just now at the six families that lived

in the constant neglect of the Sabbath. In the course of time five of these families were broken up by the separation of husbands and wives, and the sixth was brought to the same state, by the father becoming a thief. Eight or nine of the parents in those families, became drunkards; and all of them became very poor. Out of forty or fifty of their descendants, nearly one-half became drunkards, gamblers, and thoroughly wicked. Five of them were sent to the State prison, one was killed in a duel, and numbers of them had to go to the almshouse. Only one of them became a Christian, and he after having lived a very wicked life.

And now, let us look at the five families that kept the Sabbath. They were all prosperous and successful in business. A large proportion of their children became consistent members of the Church. Some of them are ruling officers in the Church; one of them is a minister, and another, a missionary to China. None of them are poor. Several of them have lived in the same home for three generations; and all of them who have died, have died in the peace and hope of the gospel. And here we see how our influence on the country in which we live, must be for good, or for evil, according as we keep, or neglect, the Sabbath.

Our next illustration may be called—

BATTLES ON THE SABBATH.

When men begin to fight on God's day, they begin by breaking His commandment, and then of course, they cannot look for success. Now, let us just take a glance into history, and see what it has to say on this subject.

General Montgomery made his attack on Quebec on the Sabbath. And what was the result? Why he was slain, and his army defeated.

In the war of the Revolution, the Americans began the battle of Monmouth on the Sabbath, and they were defeated in it.

The British began the engagement on Lake Champlain, on God's day, and they were entirely overthrown.

They began the battle of New Orleans on this day, and utter defeat attended them.

Napoleon Bonaparte commenced the battle of Waterloo, on the Sabbath, and what followed?

Why he was defeated, his army destroyed, and his empire lost.

It would be easy to multiply such examples, but these are enough to show that God's blessing does not rest on those who break the Sabbath.

We have only one other illustration here. We may call it—

THE SABBATH-KEEPING FURNACES.

Some years ago, an article was published in one of our religious papers, giving an account of some iron mills in England, where no work was allowed to be done on the Sabbath, and of the great success which attended them. Mr. Wm. E. Dodge, an earnest Christian gentleman of New York, and particularly interested in the proper observance of the Sabbath, was so pleased with this article when he read it, that he cut it out of the paper, and kept it. He was going to England the next summer, and he made up his mind to go and visit those mills, and see if the account of them was true.

One evening, during the winter after his return, Mr. Dodge was attending a meeting of the Sabbath Committee of the Cooper Institute, in

New York, when he gave an account of his visit to those mills. Mr. Dodge said he had to go a long distance out of his way, to reach those mills, but that he was well rewarded for his trouble. "In going through those parts of the country, where the mills were accustomed to work on the Sabbath," he said, " I noticed that the condition of the working people seemed poor and wretched. But, it was very different when I reached the mills, which I had gone so far to see. These belonged to the immense establishment of the Messrs Bynall, in Staffordshire. There I saw on every hand, satisfactory evidence of the existence of order, sobriety, and prosperity. On the grounds, not far from the mills, was a large building, two hundred feet long, with a boy's school at one end, and a girl's school at the other. In the middle of this building was a chapel, so arranged that the whole could be thrown into one large hall, with seats for two thousand persons, young and old; and that number was accustomed to meet there every Sabbath, for the worship of God. There are six immense furnaces belonging to this establishment. For eighteen years not a particle of iron has ever been made there on the Sabbath day; and yet, since they have been working but six days in the week, they have made more iron, with the same number of hands employed, than when they used to work seven days; and more than has been made by any other establishment of the same size in England, where work was done on the Sabbath. The owners of those mills," said Mr. Dodge, "changed the pay day of their men, from Saturday to Monday, and this removed from them, very much of the temptation to spend their money in drink on the Sabbath."

Now this is a very important statement. If there is any business which seems to make it necessary to keep at work on the Sabbath, it would seem to be that connected with the making of iron. And yet, here is a practical proof, of the most satisfactory character, and running through a period of eighteen years, that even in iron-making, by honoring the Sabbath, and working only six days in the week, instead of seven, more work can be done, and better work too, than when the fourth Commandment is broken, and the Sabbath is used as a working day. And these facts all show us, that our second reason for minding the warning against breaking the Sabbath, should be, for the sake of our country.

The third reason why we ought to mind this warning is—FOR THE LORD'S SAKE.

The first time that we hear of the Sabbath being kept, was after the creation of the world. And God himself, is the first person that we know of, who ever kept the Sabbath. In the second chapter of Genesis we read: " And on the seventh day God ended his work, which he had made, and he rested on the seventh day, from all his work which he had made. And God blessed the seventh day, and sanctified it; because that in it he had rested from all his work which God created and made."

God did not need rest, after working for six days, as we do; yet he took the rest, and kept the Sabbath day, to set us an example, about keeping this day holy. And here we have a good reason, why we should mind this warning against breaking the Sabbath. God Himself has set us an example in this matter, and we should be careful to follow this example, for the Lord's sake.

And then we have the *command of God*—as well as his example, to influence us in this matter. When the Israelites were on their march from Egypt to Canaan, God met them at Mount Sinai. Dark clouds covered the top of the mountain. The thunder roared, and the lightning flashed, and the angels' trumpets sounded from the midst of those clouds, and the mountain smoked, and trembled, because God had come down upon it. And His voice was heard proclaiming to the people the Ten Commandments. And the Fourth among these was this command, about the Sabbath. This shows us how much God is interested in this subject. If we keep the Sabbath day, we please and honor God. If we do not keep it, then we break one of His great commandments. And in doing this we displease and dishonor Him. It is just as if we should set ourselves in opposition to Him, and try to overturn His throne. How dreadful it is for poor sinful creatures, such as we are, to think of doing anything so awful as this! Yet this is what we do, when we neglect to keep the Sabbath. And here we see, that if there was no reason why we should keep the

Sabbath for our own sake,—or for the sake of our country, there is reason enough why we should do it,—for the Lord's sake. When we allow ourselves to break the Sabbath, we trample God's commandment under our feet, and declare by our actions, if not by our lips, that we are not willing to have Him for our God. The very thought of this is terrible. If we have any right feeling towards God, and any proper regard for His authority, this will lead us to keep the Sabbath day holy—for the Lord's sake.

Now, let us look at some examples of the way in which this feeling, when properly exercised, will lead us to act in reference to the Sabbath.

Our first illustration may be called—

THE DEFECTIVE MILL.

A minister of the gospel had a miller in his parish, who was very proud of his mill. It was a very busy mill. It showed no respect to the Sabbath, but went on grinding away, through all the seven days of the week. One day the minister brought a sack of wheat to the mill, to be ground into fine flour.

"A very fine mill this," said the minister, "the best I ever saw."

The miller had often heard this said, and thought it was no more than just.

"But," said the minister, "your mill has one bad defect, my friend."

"One bad defect! Pray what is that, sir?" asked the miller, in great surprise.

"It is a very serious defect," said the minister. "It is a defect which will be sure to damage the mill," continued the minister, "and will some day ruin the owner."

"Do tell me, sir, what it is," said the miller, with great earnestness.

"Your mill grinds on the *Sabbath day*," said the minister, "and in doing this, it breaks God's commandment. It dishonors him, and sets a bad example to all the people in this neighborhood."

The minister said some more kind, faithful, solemn words to his friend the miller, and then left him.

The words which the minister had spoken to the miller, touched his conscience. He thought about the great sin he had been committing.

He asked God to forgive him the wrong he had done, and then he prayed for help to do what was right in this matter.

And soon after this, to the great joy of the neighborhood, the defect in that mill, of which the minister had spoken, was remedied. It was never known to work again on the Sabbath day. And that miller was led to do this, not for his own sake, or for the sake of his country, but for the Lord's sake.

Our next incident may be called—

THE EXPERIENCE OF A CHRISTIAN WORKMAN.

"I had been in the employment of a gentleman, who kept a large machine shop, for seven years," says this man, "and never had any trouble about the Sabbath. But one Saturday evening, after paying me my wages, he said, 'John, I want you to be on hand to-morrow morning, to push forward the work on that machine, which is to go to South America.'

"'To-morrow is the Sabbath, Mr. Jones. I cannot work on the Sabbath without breaking the command of God, and doing violence to my own conscience.'

"'That is nothing to me,' said Mr Jones; 'you can stick to your principles, as much as you please, but my work must be done. If you can't do it, I shall not need your services any longer.'

"'Mr. Jones, have I ever disobliged you before? and have I not always done my work well?'

"'That is nothing to the point,' said my employer. 'I ask you to come and work to-morrow. If you do so, it will be all right. If not, I don't want you any more.'

"I dared not do as he wanted me," said this honest workman, "and so I lost my situation. This blow came upon me in the dullest season of the year. My wife and children were sick, and all the mills were discharging some of their men. But I was determined that come what might, I would not break the Sabbath.

"I spent eleven days in trying to find work, but without success. As I was going home on the evening of the eleventh day, I lifted up my heart to God; and said, 'O Lord, I have done all I can to get work, but have not succeeded. Thou hast promised that bread shall be given to thy people, and their water shall be sure. Now please open some way for me to get bread and water, for myself and family.'

"Soon after I reached home, Mr. Jones, my old employer, called to see me. He asked if I had any work yet.

"I answered, 'No, but I suppose you don't want me?'

"'Well,' said he, 'I think you were pretty stiff in your opinions. But I want you to take up that job where you left it.'

"'I will gladly do so,' was my reply. 'But I can't work on the Sabbath. I will gladly work till midnight on Saturdays, but then I must stop.'

"'All right,' said he; 'you'll never be asked to work on the Sabbath again.'"

Now, here was the case of a man who felt bound to keep the Sabbath, *for the Lord's sake.* And we see how God blessed him for what he did. The situation, which he seemed to have lost was restored to him, with the confidence and respect of his employer; and he held that situation all the rest of his days.

I have one other illustration of this part of our subject We may call it—

A PARABLE.

"O dear, I am so tired of Sunday!" said little Willie, a playful fellow of ten years old, who was longing for Monday to come, that he might again enjoy the pleasure he took in playing with his toys.

"Who wants to hear a story?" said his Uncle James, who was sitting by reading.

"I do," said Willie. "And so do I," said his brother and sister, and they all gathered round their uncle. He said, "Our Saviour, when He was on earth, used parables all the time, and so now I want to tell you a parable. It is about a kind man and his apple tree.

"The apples were hanging on this tree quite ripe, and looking very beautiful. One day a poor man, as he was passing along the road, stopped to look at this tree, and to admire the beautiful apples that hung on it. He counted the ripe golden pippins and found there were just seven of them. It made his mouth water to look at them. While he was doing this, the owner of the place came out. He was a kind-hearted man, and loved to make people happy. 'My friend,' he said, 'I'll give you some of these apples.'

"'Thank you, sir,' said the poor man, and eagerly held out his hands to receive the gift so kindly offered him. Six of the apples were placed in his hands. The owner only kept one for himself.

"Now don't you think that poor man ought to have felt very grateful for the kindness shown to him? Certainly, he should. But he did not. He wanted to have the seven apples all for himself. And at last he made up his mind that he would go back, and watch his opportunity to steal the other apple."

"And did he do that?" asked Willie, very indignantly. "The mean fellow! he ought to have been ashamed of himself. I hope he got well punished for stealing that apple."

"How many days are there in a week, Willie?" asked his uncle.

"Seven," said Willie, blushing deeply; for now he began to see the meaning of the parable, and it made him feel very uncomfortable. And well he might feel so. For when God has given us six days, out of the seven, in each week, for our own purposes, and only keeps one for Himself, isn't it mean, and wicked, in the highest degree, for us to try to rob Him of that one day? And yet this is just what we do, when we break the Sabbath day. Surely then, for the Lord's sake, we ought to mind this warning against breaking the Sabbath.

Now where is our text to-day? Exodus xx. 8. What are the words of the text? "Remember the Sabbath day to keep it holy." What is our sermon about? The warning against breaking the Sabbath.

How many reasons did we have for minding this warning? Three. In the first place, we ought to mind it, why? *For our own sake.* In the second, why? For *the sake of our country.* And in the third, why? *For the Lord's sake.*

Let it be our earnest prayer that God may help us to keep the fourth commandment, for our own sake—for the sake of our country—and for His sake; and then we shall live happy and useful lives—and lives that will be to the honor of His holy name forever.

X.

THE WARNING AGAINST PRIDE.

"Be not proud."
JEREMIAH xiii. 15.

IT is surprising how much the Bible has to say about the sin of pride, and about the proud people who give way to it. In looking carefully through the Bible, I find that there are more than a hundred places in which this sin is spoken of. Kings, and princes, and great and rich men are the ones most tempted to give way to pride. But it is not confined to them. The poorest people in the world, and those who occupy the very lowest positions in the land, are tempted to give way to pride. I have known a boy to feel proud because he had a bigger kite, or marble, than his playmate had; and I have known a little girl to feel proud because she had a prettier ribbon for her bonnet, or a nicer dress for her doll, than her companion had.

A Christian lady, who was laboring among the poor and degraded residents of the Five Points, in the city of New York, says that pride is to be met with even there. "I know one woman in my district," said this lady to a friend, "who refuses to associate with her next door neighbor, because there is only one chair in her room, while she has two in hers."

Many of the inhabitants of the valleys, that lie between the Alps in Switzerland, have large swellings, called goitres, which hang down from the sides of their necks, like great bags. They are horrible things to look at. And yet, strange as it may seem, the Swiss get to be proud even of these dreadful deformities. They look down with contempt on their neighbors who do not have these terrible swellings, and call them the "*goose-necked*" people. And so we see that pride is a sin into which we are all in danger of falling. And here in our text, we have God's warning against pride. He says to each of us—"Be not proud." And so our sermon to-day, is about—*The warning against pride*. And there are *three* things in pride, on account of which we ought all to mind this warning.

THE WARNING AGAINST PRIDE. 241

And the first thing that pride brings with it, on account of which we ought to mind this warning is— UNHAPPINESS.

A proud person never can be happy, no matter how rich and great he may be. We have a striking illustration of this, in the book of Esther, in the Old Testament. There we read about Ahasuerus, the king of Persia, and the eastern part of the world. He was the greatest king then known. He had a great number of servants and officers under him. At the head of all these was a man whose name was Haman. He was the prime minister of that great kingdom; and his riches and honors were such, that as he walked to and from the palace of the king, the people who met him were accustomed to bow their heads, and make obeisance to him. And every time this was done it helped to make him prouder still. But there was one man, named Mordecai, a Jew, who never would do this. He was the uncle of Esther, the wife of the king, and used to sit near the gate of the king's palace. And as he saw Haman pass by, he would not bow to him, or take any notice of him. This wounded Haman's pride, and made him feel very unhappy. On reaching home one day, after passing Mordecai, who had refused to bow to him, he was very angry. He spoke about it to some of his friends there. He told them of all the riches, and honors, which the king had bestowed upon him, but said that he could not enjoy any of these, so long as Mordecai the Jew would not bow down and make obeisance to him. Here we see, what unhappiness Haman's pride brought upon him. And this is the way in which it always acts.

Here are some other illustrations of the unhappiness which pride occasions.

In one of Æsop's fables, we have a good illustration of this part of our subject. It is the fable of the tortoise and the eagle.

The fable says, that there was a tortoise once, that was very unhappy, because he had no wings, and could not fly. He used to look up and see the eagles and other birds, spreading out their wings, and having a good time, as they went floating through the air. He said to himself, "Oh, if I only had wings, as those birds have, so that I could rise up into the air, and sail about there as they do, how happy I should be!"

THE WARNING AGAINST PRIDE. 243

One day, the fable says, he called to an eagle, and offered him a great reward if he would only teach him how to fly. " I never shall be happy," said the tortoise, "till I get wings, and am able to fly about in the air as you do." The eagle told him he had no wings to give him, and did not know how to teach him to fly. But the tortoise pressed him so earnestly, and made him so many promises, that finally the eagle said— "Well, I'll try what I can do. You get on my back, and I'll carry you up into the air, and we'll see what can be done."

So the tortoise got on the back of the eagle. Then the eagle spread out his wings, and began to soar aloft. He went up, and up, and up, till he had reached a great height. Then he said to the tortoise: " Now, get ready. I'm going to throw you off, and you must try your hand at flying." So the eagle threw him off; and he went down, down, down, till at last he fell upon a hard rock, and was dashed to pieces.

Now here you see, it was the pride of the tortoise which made him so unhappy, because he couldn't fly. And it was trying to gratify his pride which cost him his life.

I have one other illustration of this part of our sermon. We may call it—

MOVING MOUNTAINS.

"Mamma," said a little girl to her mother one day, "if people can move mountains by faith—why don't they do it now?"

"They do, sometimes, Lucy dear. I knew a little girl once, who moved a very big one out of my way."

"Oh! mamma, do tell me all about it," said Lucy.

"Well, when I was about ten years old, I went to a pretty village to spend the summer. Of course I went to the Sunday School, while I was there, and I liked all the girls in our class very much, except one, whose name was Jessie Muir. Jessie was the plainest dressed girl in our class, because her mother was very poor; but she always knew her lessons perfectly, and the teacher loved her very much.

The summer was passing away, and I had hardly spoken a dozen words to Jessie. One Sunday, at the close of school, our teacher told us, that our lesson for next Sunday, would be about "moving mountains," and she wished us to study it carefully. But I was very busy with other things that week, and I never thought about the lesson, till Sunday morning came. Then I had to have my breakfast, and get dressed, and there was no time to study the lesson.

"After breakfast I was hurrying to start for school, with my new blue silk dress on, and my white straw hat. But I was thinking more of what the girls would say of my nice new dress, than about the lesson. Just as I went out of the gate into the lane, Jessie Muir was going by. It was quite a walk to church. I felt as if I would like to be kind to somebody, so I said—"Good morning, Jessie." "Good morning," she answered, pleasantly. After we had walked together a little while, she asked—"Have you learned your lesson?"

"No," I said, "I can't make anything out of it; can you?"

"Yes, I can make three things out of it," said Jessie.

"Can you? And what are they?"

"The *first* is—that we must have faith in the power of Jesus. The *second* is, that we are not to move mountains of earth. And the *third* is, that there are mountains we must move, if we are true Christians, and hope to be happy ourselves, and to make others happy."

"What do you mean by that, Jessie?" I asked, in a pettish sort of way.

"Why just this; that every sin is a mountain in our way to heaven; and some of them are not mountains to us alone, but to our friends about us."

I felt my face getting red, as I said, "I suppose you see a great many mountains in me?"

"It is always easy to see others' faults," said Jessie. "Do you want me to tell you hat I think is your greatest?"

"Well," I said, with a touch of anger—"pray what is it?"

"It is pride," said Jessie, in a very gentle way. "Don't you want to move it, Annie?"

"I don't know how," I said, in a low voice.

"'Whatsoever ye shall ask the Father in my name, He will do it,' are the words of Jesus. O, Annie, I wish you would ask Him to help you remove this mountain."

"I guess it don't make any difference to you,

THE WARNING AGAINST PRIDE. 247

Jessie, whether I get rid of my pride or not."

"Yes, it does, Annie, for you have no right to be a mountain in my way."

"I am not," I answered angrily.

"Yes, you are, Annie: for when I see you proud and scornful, I know you are unhappy yourself, and it makes me feel unhappy too. You make me feel discontented with my lot, because I can't have the things that you have: and you make me feel unkind towards you. And I have no doubt that some of the other girls feel just the same way."

We had reached the church door as Jessie finished those words. I had no time to say anything more to her then. But I never forgot what she had said. It led me to see my sin in giving way to pride. Then I asked Jesus to help me remove this mountain out of my way. He did so. And then I was no longer unhappy myself; and was not the means of making others unhappy by giving way to pride. That little girl had learned the Bible warning against pride. And the first reason why we ought to mind this warning—is that pride brings with it—unhappiness.

The second reason why we ought to mind this warning, is that pride brings with it—TROUBLE.

We never can set ourselves against any of God's laws without getting into trouble. Here, in our text, we have God's law, regarding pride. He says to us—"*Be not proud.*" If we mind this law, we shall have pleasure in what we do. If we do not mind this law we shall have trouble. It is impossible for us to go contrary to any of God's laws, without finding trouble. Here is a very simple illustration of what I am saying. Suppose that you and I, are sitting on the sofa, in our parlor. We have a favorite pussy cat. She comes and lies down on the sofa between us. How nice and clean she looks, and how smooth and glossy her hair is! Now the law of God is that pussy's hair shall grow in the direction from her head, down towards her tail. And if you lay your hand on her back, and stroke her hair down in that direction, how nice and smooth it will feel! Stroking in that way, will give only pleasure, both to pussy and yourself. She will lie there, and purr away, to show you how happy she is. But suppose that instead of this, you try to stroke her in the opposite direction. *That* would be contrary to God's law for stroking cats. It would only give trouble, both to pussy and yourself. She would stop purring, and jump down from the sofa, and run away, saying as plainly as she could, by her actions, "I don't like to be stroked in that way."

And it is the same with all God's laws. If we act according to them, it will cause us pleasure. If we act contrary to them, it will cause us trouble. And this is just as true, in regard to God's law concerning pride, as it is in anything else. God says to each of us—"Be not proud." This is His law about pride. If we mind this law, and walk humbly before Him, not thinking of ourselves more highly than we ought to think, we shall find pleasure in so doing; but if we give way to pride, and break God's law, it will be sure to cause us trouble. Let us look at some illustrations of this.

The book of Daniel gives us a good illustration, in what we read in the 4th chapter, about Nebuchadnezzar. He was king of Babylon, then the mightiest kingdom in the world. He had surrounded the city with vast walls, and had built splendid palaces and temples in it. And when he thought of all his riches, and his grandeur, it made him feel very proud; and the more he thought about it, the more his pride increased. Qne day, as he was walking in his splendid palace, he said to himself—" Is not this great Babylon, that I have built, by the might of my power, and for the honor of my majesty?" And as he thought about all this, his pride went on increasing till it unsettled his mind, and he became crazy. They had no asylums for insane people then, as we have now; and they did not know what to do with them. So Nebuchadnezzar, the great king, was driven out from his palace, and his home, to live with the wild beasts of the field. We are told that—" he did eat grass as oxen, and his body was wet with the dew of heaven, till his hairs were grown like eagles' feathers, and his nails like birds' claws." This continued for seven long years. Then it pleased God to make him well again, and he was restored to his kingdom. But how fearful was the trouble which Nebuchadnezzar's pride brought upon him!

Our next story may be called—

TWO KINDS OF LADIES.

An earnest Christian lady, engaged as a Bible reader, was hastening along State street in Boston, one bleak November day, when she saw a lame, deformed boy, coming towards her, carrying several bundles in his arms. His dress was thin and poor. His limbs twisted in a very strange way, as he walked. Just before this lady came up to the poor crippled boy, he stumbled, and dropped one of his bundles, which broke, and emptied a string of sausages on the side walk.

Two richly dressed ladies, then passing by, held up their silken skirts, and looked scornfully on the lame boy, as one of them said to the other—"What a horrid creature!"

Several other ladies, in going by, looked proudly down on the poor lame boy, and without giving him one kind look, or word, went on their way, laughing at him in his misery.

This made the boy feel very badly. The pride of those gayly dressed females, who called themselves *ladies*, caused him a great deal of trouble. He stopped to pick up the sausages, but in doing this, he let another parcel fall. Then he stopped and looked in despair at his lost parcels, with the feeling that he never could get them again.

Then this good Bible reader, with her bright face, stepped to the boy's side, and said in the kindest possible way: "Here, my little man, let me hold those bundles while you pick up what you have lost."

Dumb with surprise, the poor fellow handed them over to his kind friend, and then gathered up what had fallen. Then the good lady tied them up safely with a strong piece of string, and placing them in the poor boy's crooked arms, said with an encouraging smile—

"I hope you haven't far to go, my friend."

He was overwhelmed with astonishment, at all this kindness; and looking with wonder at his good friend, he said:

"Be you a lady?"

"I hope so; I try to be," was her reply.

"I was kind of hoping you wasn't."

"Why so?" she asked, with a good deal of surprise.

"'Cause I've seen such as called themselves

ladies, but they never spoke a kind and pleasant word to me, or any 'cepting the granduns. I guess there's two kinds—them as thinks they's ladies but isn't, and them as tries to be, and is."

Now here, we see what trouble was caused to that poor crippled boy, by the pride of those well-dressed females, who refused to show him any kindness; and what happiness he found from the treatment of that good Christian lady, who had learned the lesson God teaches us, when he says, "Be not proud."

Here is one other illustration of this part of our subject: we may call it—

TOO PROUD TO TAKE ADVICE.

Two masons were engaged in building a brick wall, in front of a high house. One of them was older and more experienced than his companion. The younger one, whose name was Ben, placed a brick in the wall which was thicker at one end than at the other. His companion noticed it, and said—"Ben, if I were you I wouldn't leave that brick there. It's not straight, and will be likely to injure the wall by making it untrue."

"Pooh!" said Ben, "what difference will such a trifle as that make? You are too particular."

"My mother used to teach me," said his friend, "that truth is truth; and that ever so little an untruth is a lie, and that a lie is no trifle."

Now Ben was a proud young fellow. His pride was offended by what his friend had said to him.

So he straightened himself up, and said in an angry tone—

"Well, I guess I understand my business as well as you do. I am sure that brick wont do any harm."

His friend said nothing more to him. They both went quietly on with their work, laying one brick after another, and carrying the wall up higher, till the close of the day. Then they quitted their work and went home.

The next morning, they went back to go on with their work again. But when they got there, they found the wall all in ruins. The explanation of it was this: that uneven brick had given it a little slant. As the wall got up higher, the slant increased, till at last, in the middle of the night, it tumbled over and fell down to the ground.

And here we see the trouble which this young man brought on himself by his pride. If he had only learned to mind this Bible warning against it, that wall would not have fallen down, and he would have been saved the trouble of building it up again. The second reason why we ought to mind this warning, is because pride brings trouble with it.

The third reason why we ought to mind this warning is, that pride brings with it—LOSS.

The apostle tells us that "God resisteth the proud, but giveth grace to the humble." So if we give way to pride, we are in a position in which God is resisting us, and then it is certain, that we can expect nothing but loss, in every thing that we do. In the words of our text, God says to us, "Be not proud." This is His command to us concerning pride. David tells us that "in keeping His commandments there is great reward." But if we give way to pride we are breaking one of God's commands, and then of course, we shall lose the great reward He promises to those who keep His commands.

When we begin to love and serve God, He says to each of us, "from this day will I bless thee." And we are told that "the blessing of the Lord maketh rich, and he addeth no sorrow." The riches which this blessing brings us, do not mean gold and silver, and earthly property. The way in which God's blessing makes His people rich, is in the peace, and joy, and happiness which He gives them; in the sense of His favor, and the protection which they have in this world, and in the hope of sharing His presence and glory forever in heaven. But if we give way to pride, we cannot love and serve God; and then we must lose the blessing which God promises to those who do love and serve Him. And *this*, is the greatest loss we can ever meet with in this world. To those who truly serve Him, God promises that He will "make all things work together for their good." This is one of the most precious promises to be found in the Bible. But if we give way to pride, we cannot love God; and then we must lose that sweet promise; and nobody can calculate how great that loss would be. We read in another place—that —"pride goeth before destruction." The word

THE WARNING AGAINST PRIDE.   257

"destruction" here used, is a very comprehensive word. It takes in a great deal. It means the destruction or loss of our peace—our happiness—our prosperity in this world; and in the world to come—the loss of our souls—the loss of heaven. And can we think of any loss equal to this? Now let us look at some illustrations of the great loss that comes from pride.

We have our first illustration in the case of the angels.

I refer particularly now to those angels that—"kept not their first estate." We speak of them as—"the *fallen* angels." They were made just like the other angels. They were as pure, as holy, as happy, as perfect as angels could be. God was their Father, and heaven was their home. They had the prospect before them, of being perfectly happy forever. But, somehow or other, we know not how, they gave way to pride. They were unwilling any longer to obey God. Then we are told that "there was war in heaven." And the end of it was, that they were cast down from heaven to hell. Their pride cost them the loss of heaven.

We have our next illustration in the case of

Adam and Eve. God made them perfect, and put them in the Garden of Eden as their home. There they had everything around them to make them perfectly happy. They did as they wished, and went where they pleased in that beautiful garden. God told them that they might eat of all the trees of the garden except one: but of that they must not eat. *This* was the only command they had to mind. That made their situation very easy. But Satan got into that garden. He came and tempted them to eat of that tree. He told them that if they would only eat of it, they would become as wise as gods. This kindled their pride. They felt that they would like above all things, to be made like gods. This thought led them to break the one command which God had given them, and to eat of the fruit of that forbidden tree. The result was that they were driven out of Paradise. Their pride caused them the loss of that beautiful garden.

Our next illustration we have in the case of Saul, the first king of Israel. There had been no king in his family before him. His father was only a farmer. But one time, some of his asses had wandered away and got lost. Saul was sent

THE WARNING AGAINST PRIDE. 259

out to try and find them. After hunting for them a long time in vain, he was at a loss what to do. So he made up his mind to call on the prophet Samuel, and ask for information about the lost asses. Samuel told him not to give himself any more trouble about them, as they had been found. Then Samuel took him aside, and told him that God had chosen him to be king over Israel, and had given him, Samuel, direction to anoint him king. He did so. Thus Saul was made king of Israel. And if he had only minded this warning against pride, there never would have been any other kings of Israel, but the descendants of Saul. But he became proud. His pride kept him from doing what God told him to do. And for this reason, God took the kingdom from Saul, and gave it to David. And so we see, how Saul's pride brought upon him the loss of his kingdom.

Now where is our text to-day? Jeremiah xiii. 15. What are the words of the text? "Be not proud." What is the sermon about? The warning against pride.

How many things are there in pride, on account of which we ought to mind this warning? Three things.

What is the first thing that pride brings with it, on account of which we ought to mind this warning? Unhappiness. What is the second thing? Trouble. What is the third thing? Loss.

Jesus, our blessed Saviour, "came to visit us in great humility." And if we pray for grace to be like him, and to—" tread in the blessed steps of his most holy life," it is very certain that we shall mind the warning of our text—

"BE NOT PROUD."

XI.

THE WARNING AGAINST SLOTHFULNESS.

"Be ye not slothful."—HEBREWS vi. 12.

SLOTHFULNESS is the same as idleness. An idle person is one who neglects his duty, and who never can succeed in anything. Solomon says that—"slothfulness," or idleness—"will clothe a man with rags." We need not wonder therefore, to find among the warnings of the Bible, one against idleness, or slothfulness. And God, who gives us this warning, has set before us many splendid examples of industry, which is the opposite of slothfulness, or idleness. See what an example of this we have in God Himself. When our Saviour was on earth, he said to the Jews,—"My Father *worketh hitherto,* and I work." This means, that from the time when God made our world, and all the worlds in the universe, thousands on thousands of years ago,

He has been steadily working on all the while. He is occupied, day and night, in governing, and taking care of all these worlds. There is no slothfulness, or idleness about Him.

And then think of the angels of heaven. They wait before God continually to do His bidding. And the moment He tells them to go anywhere, or do anything, they fly away and do it. There is no slothfulness, or idleness among the angels. And then think of the Sun. God made it, thousands of years ago, by its shining to light up our world, and the worlds around it. And since then it has kept on shining day and night, without ever stopping for a moment. There is no slothfulness, or idleness about the sun. And so it is with the moon, and the stars, and the seasons, and day and night. There is no slothfulness, or idleness about any of them. They all mind the warning that God has given about idleness. And this is our subject to-day. The words of our text are—"Be ye not slothful." Here we have the—*Bible warning against slothfulness.*

And there are *three* good reasons, why we ought to mind this warning.

THE WARNING AGAINST SLOTHFULNESS. 263

The first reason why we ought to mind this warning is—FOR THE SAKE OF OUR EXAMPLE.

One of the most powerful influences that any of us can exert on those around us, either for good or for evil, is the influence of example. The most powerful preacher in the world, cannot be always preaching with his voice. But by our example, we are preaching all the time, wherever we may go. If we are Christians, and are trying to keep God's commandments, then by our example, we are exerting an influence that will help others to do the same. But if we are living in idleness, and so are neglecting the warning God gives us in our text, then we are doing all we can to lead others to be idle too. Let us look at some illustrations of the good that has been done, by those who have minded this warning, and were setting the right example to those about them, on this subject. Our first illustration may be called—

THE PRINTER'S BOY

About the year 1725, an American boy, nineteen years old, found himself in London, where he had to earn his own bread. He went one day to a printing office, and asked for employment.

"Where are you from?" asked the foreman.

"From America," was the answer.

"Ah!" said the foreman, "from America! a lad from America seeking employment as a printer! Well, do you really understand the art of printing? Can you set type?"

The young man stepped up to one of the type-cases, and in a short time set up the following passage, from St. John's Gospel, which he handed to the foreman—"Nathaniel said unto him, Can there any good thing come out of Nazareth? Philip saith unto him, Come and see."

The foreman was so pleased with the readiness and smartness of this American youth, that he took him into his employ at once. He was very industrious, and soon gained the confidence and respect of all connected with the office. He was always in his place, and did his work well. He never would drink beer, or strong drink. He saved his money, and after awhile returned to his own country. Then he had a printing establishment of his own. He became an author, a publisher, the Postmaster-General of the country,—a member of Congress,—a signer of the Declaration of Independence, and an ambassador from his country to some of the royal courts of Europe, and finally he died in Philadelphia, on the 17th of April, 1790, at the age of eighty-four, full of years and honors.

This was *Benjamin Franklin.* No one can tell the influence which his example for industry has had upon thousands of the youth of our country. But we may form a pretty fair idea of this when we bear in mind that there are more than a hundred and fifty counties, towns, and villages that have been called—*Franklin,* in honor of this industrious printer's boy.

Our next story may be called—

BERTIE'S INDUSTRY, OR—"I CAN, BECAUSE I OUGHT."

Bertie was a boy about twelve years old, with not a bit of idleness connected with him. One afternoon he was working away among his books, trying to get his arithmetic lesson for the next day, when his uncle Jim called to him, saying,—"Bertie, don't you want to take a walk? Your brother Sam and I are going down to the river."

Bertie started eagerly, on hearing this call, and upset his chair in the hurry. But recovering himself in a moment, he picked up his chair, and sat down again to his studies, saying as he did so: "No, thank you, Uncle Jim. I should like to go very much, but I can't do anything till I have finished my lessons."

"What a goose you are, Bert," said his brother Sam, as he stowed his books into his desk, with great eagerness. "How you can stay bothering over those musty-fusty old books, when you have the chance of a splendid walk with uncle Jim, I'm sure I can't understand."

"*I can, because I ought,*" was Bertie's quiet answer, as he turned to his books.

Uncle Jim heard what Bertie said—"I can, because I ought," and the words had a great effect upon him. He kept thinking of them all the afternoon, as he was walking with his nephew Sam. He thought of them the last thing at night, when he went to bed, and the first thing as he woke in the morning. He had never learned to practice the Bible warning against idleness. "I can, because I ought." "Has this been my rule of life?" he asked himself. He

THE WARNING AGAINST SLOTHFULNESS.

felt that it had not been, but that it *ought* to be. He resolved to make it so. He prayed to God to help him. And the end of it was, that the example of his nephew Bertie, in minding the Bible warning against idleness, and saying, "I can, because I ought," ended in bringing his Uncle Jim to the Saviour, and leading him to become an earnest and devoted Christian. And here we see, that one reason why we ought to mind this warning against slothfulness, is for the sake of our example.

The second reason why we ought to mind this warning is—FOR OUR SUCCESS IN LIFE.

When we learn to mind this warning, it will make us diligent and industrious, in all the work we have to do ; and it is *this*, that will make us successful, in anything we undertake. A lady once asked Mr. Turner, the great English painter, what the secret of his success was ? His reply was: "I have no secret, madam, but *hard work*." "The difference between one man and another," says Dr. Arnold, "is not so much in talent, as in industry." "Nothing," says Sir Joshua Reynolds, "is denied to well directed labor, and nothing is to be attained without it." "Success," says Dr. Johnson, "may be won by patient industry, but it is not to be looked for in any other way." Solomon says—"The hand of the diligent maketh rich." Again he says, "seest thou a man diligent in his business; he shall stand before kings, he shall not stand before mean men."

Periander, one of the seven wise men of Greece, wrote a motto, which was inscribed on the walls of the celebrated temple of Delphos, in these words—

"*Nothing is impossible to industry.*"

The famous battle of Waterloo, was one of the most important battles ever fought, because it put an end to the power of Napoleon Bonaparte, and the terrible loss of life, which that power had occasioned. It was the great Duke of Wellington, one of England's most celebrated heroes, who won that battle. In the latter part of his life, he visited the well-known school at Eton, where he had studied when a boy, and was asked to make an address to the students of that school. He did so, and in closing his address, he said: "My young friends, I want you always to remember this, *that the battle of*

THE WARNING AGAINST SLOTHFULNESS. 269

Waterloo was gained at Eton." What he meant by this was, that it was the warning against idleness, which he had learned and practiced there, that led to the success of his after life. And if we learn and practice that lesson while we are young, it will have the same effect on us. Now let us look at some other illustrations of this part of our subject. Our first story may be called—

DILIGENCE REWARDED.

A good many years ago, a little boy entered the Harrow School in England. He was put into a class beyond his years. The other boys in the class had been prepared for it, by going through some studies which he had never been taught. The consequence was that he was at the tail of the class. He found it hard work to keep up with the other boys, and the teacher would scold him every day, for not knowing his lessons better. Now many a boy would have been discouraged by such an experience, and have given up trying. But it was not so with this boy. He made up his mind that he would get the grammar, and the other books which his classmates had gone through with, and never rest till he had mastered them. He did so. He gave up his play-hours, and many of his sleeping hours, to this work. This soon began to tell on his lessons. He left his place at the tail of his class, and went up, step by step, till he got to the head of it. He became the foremost scholar in the school, and was appointed what they called the dux, or leader of his division, and the Harrow School was proud of him.

And that boy, who had such hard work at the beginning of his studies—now has a marble statue to his memory, in the great Cathedral of St. Paul's, London. He lived to be the greatest Oriental scholar of modern Europe; and his name —Sir William Jones— is honored, and revered by men of learning all over the world. And the great success of his life resulted from his having learned, and practised, the Bible warning against slothfulness. Our next story may be called—

WILLING TO SHOVEL.

Some years ago, a young man came to this country from England, to take a position as clerk, in a new business enterprise that had been started in the south-west. He had been well educated at home, and had learned the warning against slothfulness. But when he reached the place which he had expected to make his home, he found, to his surprise and sorrow, that some unlooked for change had occurred, and the business had failed. There he was, without friends, without a home, and without money, in a strange land. He managed to work his way back to New York. He found himself an unknown stranger in the midst of that great busy city. It was midwinter; and the first morning after his arrival, he set out to find work. He was accustomed to the use of the pen, but made up his mind, if it was necessary, to use the shovel.

It was a snowy morning, and as he passed down Fourth Avenue, he saw a lot of men shovelling snow from the sidewalks. He asked permission to join them in their labor. This was granted him, and he went to work as heartily, as though shovelling had been his regular employment. Not long after this, the owner of the large store, from the front of which the snow was being shovelled, and who was a very rich man, was passing that way. He saw the young stranger's face, and was pleased with his bright intelligent look. He wondered how it happened that such a gentlemanly looking young man, should be occupied in shovelling snow. He spoke to him, and received a very kind, and respectful answer. Then he asked him some questions, so as to find out a little about his history and circumstances. He was so much pleased with what he saw and heard of this young man, that he invited him to call at his office the next day. That night the young man laid aside his shovel, which he was not to use any more.

After breakfast the next morning, he called at the rich merchant's office. There was a vacant place in his large establishment, and this was offered to the young man, who was willing industriously to use the shovel, when he could find nothing else to do. It was a poor place, with a small salary; but he filled it so well, that in a few months, he was raised to a higher position; and at the end of three years, he was the chief clerk in that great establishment, with a very large salary. He is there to-day, with the certainty that before long, if he lives, he will be a partner in one of the wealthiest mercantile houses in our country. And that young man owes his great success in life, to his having learned, and practised, the Bible warning against slothfulness.

Here are some lines, which take in all I have been trying to say on this point of our subject. They are headed—

BE IN TIME.

Be in time for every call;
If you can, be first of all;
   Be in time!
If your teachers do but find
You are never once behind,
But are like the dial, true,
They will always trust in you.
   Be in time!

Never linger ere you start;
Ever go with willing heart;
   Be in time!
In the morning up and on,
First to work, and soonest done:
This is how the goal's attained;
This the way the prize is gained;
   Be in time!

> Those who aim at something great
> Never yet were found too late;
>   Be in time!
> Life to all is but a school;
> We must work by plan and rule:
> With some noble end in view,
> Ever steady, earnest, true,
>   Be in time!

And so we see, that the second reason why we ought to mind this warning against slothfulness, is for our success in life.

The third reason why we ought to mind it is— FOR OUR REWARD IN HEAVEN.

We have seen from our last point, how by minding this warning against slothfulness, we secure to ourselves a good reward in this world. But more than this, it will also secure a brighter and more blessed reward for us in heaven. Jesus says, of every one who tries to do any work for Him—"Thou shalt be recompensed at the resurrection of the just." He says again that—"if we give a cup of cold water even, to one of the least of His followers, we shall in no wise lose our reward." And in another place He says—"Do good; and your reward shall be great in heaven." But what the greatness of

THE WARNING AGAINST SLOTHFULNESS.

our reward in heaven will be, must depend on what we do for Jesus in our present life. In the parable of the talents—which is intended to show us how God will deal with us in the day of judgment—we are told that the servant who had gained ten talents, was appointed to rule over ten cities. He who had gained five, was appointed over five; and he who had gained two, was appointed over two. And so the apostle Paul tells us, that in heaven—" every man shall receive his own reward, according to his own labor."

If we get to heaven at all, we shall owe it entirely to the grace and love of Jesus. But what our place in heaven shall be, when we get there, will be decided according to the way in which we have served Jesus on earth. St. Paul tells us that when Jesus shall come again, He will give a crown of glory to each of his people. But what kind of a crown each of us shall receive, and how many jewels there will be in it, must depend on the way in which we have served Him in this life. And this is a good reason why we should mind the warning against slothfulness.

Let us look now at some illustrations of this part of our subject.

The first may be called—

THE PRISONER'S PIN.

Some years ago a Polish Count was put in prison. He had not done anything wrong, but some political matter led to his imprisonment. He was shut up alone in a dark dungeon. Not a ray of light ever entered there, except when his keeper came in twice a day, with a lantern, bringing his meals to him. All alone in the dark, with no one to speak to, and nothing to do, how sad and dreary his life was! If he could only have had light in his cell, and some books to read, he would not have cared for the confinement. But with nothing to see, and nothing to do, he felt as if he must either grow crazy, or die. One day, as he was mourning over his sad lot, he laid his hand on the breast of his coat, and there he found a pin. This made him feel happy, and he really shouted for joy. But, why?—you may ask. What good could a poor, little, common pin do to a prisoner, alone in a dungeon? Why he felt that it would give him occupation; and this was just what he needed. He took the pin, and threw it away from him. Then he got down on his hands and knees, and went feeling round for the pin. It took him a long time to find it; but at last he succeeded. Then he felt very glad. And through the long weary time of his confinement, he used to have a hunt for that pin several times a day. This gave him exercise. It helped him to sleep, and kept him in good health.

One day, after six long years had been spent in that dungeon, his prison door was opened, and he was set at liberty. He returned to his home, in the castle which belonged to him. How happy the countess, his wife, and the children were, to welcome him back again!

The day after he was set at liberty he sent for a jeweller in the neighboring town. When he came, he gave him the pin, which had been such a comfort to him in prison, and told him to make a splendid gold breast pin, with this pin in the middle of it, surrounded with a row of the finest diamonds. He did so, and brought it to the Count. Then he presented it to the Countess his wife. She was delighted with the sight of the gold and the diamonds. But when she saw a small common pin in the centre of it, she asked what that meant. Then the Count told her the story of that pin, and what it had done for him in the prison. When he got through with it, the tears were streaming down the face of his wife. She clasped the breastpin to her bosom, and said—" This is the most precious treasure I have. I'll never part with it while I live."

And so, the work we do for Jesus on earth, when we get to heaven, like that jewelled pin to the Countess, will be the most precious jewel in the crown of our rejoicing. Our next illustration is about—

THREE EARNEST CHRISTIANS.

These were English females, and they set us splendid examples of working for Jesus. One of them was named Miss Rye. All the money she had was a little over $3000. In the use made of this money, with assistance from others, she helped 178 Christian females to go out to different British colonies, where they have all, through her efforts, found good situations. She has put 1500 English women into good places as domestics, in Australia and New Zealand.

She has herself, personally, taken to Canada, and placed in respectable families there, 1200 children, gathered from the streets of London. Nine-tenths of them were girls, who but for the efforts of this kind friend, would probably all have gone to ruin.

What a noble work that was!

The next of these good workers was a Miss Chandler. She made up her mind to try and help the poor people whose limbs were paralyzed. There was no home, or asylum, for this class of sufferers in all London then. She began her work by taking care of one poor, paralyzed carpenter. As fast as she could, she took charge of other sufferers of the same class, one by one. She has now opened a large hospital for sufferers of this kind, in Queen's Square, London. There is no better institution of this kind in the world. She has also established a hospital for convalescents, which is doing a great deal of good. She has also secured money enough, the interest of which will support permanently forty-eight patients in this hospital, free of charge. And now she is collecting a large sum of money for the purpose of supporting more free patients in this hospital.

That too is a noble work.

The third of these good workers is Miss Gilbert. She is a blind lady, and began her work by hiring a cellar in Holborn, London, for which she paid eighteen pence a week. In this cellar she began a school for the blind. She has gone steadily on with her work, for a number of years, and now she has a large school built, and paid for, in which there are a thousand pupils, whom she has taught to support themselves. They maintain that institution at a cost of $40,000 a year, and they find in it a home—an education—and employment.

These three noble women had learned, and practised, the warning against slothfulness. And for the good work they have done, how glorious their reward in heaven will be! How splendid the jewels that will sparkle in the crowns of their rejoicing! Who of us would not wish to have crowns of glory in heaven, like those which these noble women will wear?

I have one other illustration of this part of our subject. We may call it—

THE POOR BOY AND THE PREACHER.

More than a hundred years ago, a poor boy was born in a small town in England. He was the youngest of seven children. His father died when he was an infant, leaving his family without anything to live on. This boy's name was George. As soon as he was able to work, he did everything he could to help to support his mother. He became a Christian while he was quite young, and had a great desire to obtain an education. But he had no money to get it with. Yet by working at different things, and spending his evenings in hard study, he managed in the course of time, to get through the Grammar School, in the town where he lived. When he was about eighteen years old he entered one of the colleges at Oxford. But he was so poor that he had to engage himself as a servant in the college, so as to earn, in this way, the money that was needed to pay his expenses. This made it very hard for him. But in spite of all this trouble, he struggled manfully on, till he had finished his education. And though he had so much trouble to meet with, all through his college course, yet he graduated at last with great honor. But, under the circumstances in which he was placed, he never could have done this, if he had not learned and practiced the Bible warning against slothfulness. But he had done this most successfully. There was no slothfulness about him. Untiring industry was the chief element of his character.

And when he had finished his studies, he entered the ministry. He was ordained in the Church of England, but afterwards entered the Methodist Church. The person of whom I am now speaking, was the celebrated George Whitfield. He was the most eloquent and successful minister ever known in the Church of Christ, since the days of the great apostle Paul. Such crowds of people flocked to hear him, that no church building was large enough to hold them. Then he had to preach out in the open air. Congregations of twenty, or thirty thousand people, would assemble to hear him preach. And sometimes as many as fifty thousand, have met to hear him at one time. He travelled all through

England, and Scotland, again and again, preaching to such congregations as these. He visited America a number of times, preaching in the same way. Every sermon he preached, and every word he spoke, was like a seed sown by him, and in the glorious reward awaiting him in heaven, he will reap the rich harvest of his faithful sowing, through all eternity.

And here we see that we ought to mind this Bible warning against slothfulness, because of the reward it will bring to us in heaven.

Now where is our text to-day? Hebrews vi. 12. What are the words of the text? "Be ye not slothful." What is the sermon about? The Bible warning against slothfulness. How many reasons did we have for minding this warning? *Three.* The first was what? *For the sake of our example.* The second was what? *For our success in life.* And the third was what? *For our reward in heaven.* We cannot do this of ourselves; but we must ask God to help us, if we hope to be successful in serving Him. In the language of one of our beautiful Collects, let us ask God to " give us the help of His grace, that we may so faithfully serve Him in this life, that we fail not finally to attain His heavenly promises, through Jesus Christ our Lord."

"BE YE NOT SLOTHFUL."

XII.

WARNING AGAINST DISCONTENT.

" Be content with such things as ye have."
HEBREWS xiii. 5.

WHEN we feel contented, we are happy. Contentment is the health of our minds. And health should always bring comfort or happiness to us. We know how it is with our bodies. When they are in a healthy state, we find pleasure in walking, or in working, or in every movement of our limbs. But if our limbs are broken, or swollen with gout, or rheumatism, then every motion that we make, will only cause us pain and suffering. And it is just the same with our minds, as it is with our bodies. If they are in a proper, healthy state, every exercise that we make of them, will give us pleasure or comfort. But if they are in an unhealthy state, then every exercise of them, will only cause us pain and suffering. Now if we have—"learned in whatsoever state we are, to be therewith content," then our minds will be in a healthy state, and it will give us pleasure to use them in thinking about our daily duties and engagements. But, if we are discontented, then our minds are in an unhealthy state, and whatever we think about, will make us feel uncomfortable. And this shows us how important the duty is, to which the text calls our attention.

The subject we have now to consider is—*the Bible warning against discontent.* And I wish to speak of THREE good reasons why we should learn to mind this warning.

We ought to mind it, in the first place—FOR OUR OWN COMFORT.

Now suppose that you have a long walk to take every day, but you have a thorn run into your foot, or a sharp stone in your shoe,—could you have any comfort, in taking that daily walk? Certainly not. If you wished to walk with any comfort, the first thing for you to do would be to take off your shoe, and throw away the sharp stone that was in it; and then to have that thorn taken out of your foot. You never could have the least comfort in walking till this

THE WARNING AGAINST DISCONTENT. 287

was done. But a feeling of discontent in our minds, is just like that thorn in the foot, or that stone in the shoe. It will take away from us all the comfort we might have, as we go on in the walk of our daily duties.

And if we wish to have any comfort ourselves, in what we have to do, we must get rid of this feeling of discontent from our own minds. A discontented person can have no comfort in anything.

Now let us look at some illustrations of the effect of discontent on those who give way to it; and of the comfort that comes to us when we learn to practice the Bible warning against it. Our first illustration may be called—

THE FABLE OF THE DISCONTENTED BITTERN.

The bittern is a large bird, with a long neck, and long legs, that lives in swamps. The fable says, that a bittern was discontented with his condition. He had got tired of living in swamps, and eating frogs, and worms, and all sorts of reptiles. He wanted to live in the orchard like a robin, and be a favorite with every body. "I guess bitterns can sing as well as robins," he said to himself one day;—" and I have no notion of being confined to a marsh, and catching fever and ague all my days." So he started for the orchard, partly flying and running, as fast as he could go. When he got there, he began at once to build him a nest, like the robin, on the branch of an apple tree. The next day, as he was busy with this work, a farmer from a cottage near by, saw him. He got his gun and shot him. The shot did not kill him, but it broke his wing. Then he was glad to hobble back to his old home in the swamp, and to eating frogs and worms again. His discontent had taken away all his comfort. But the lesson he learned that day took away his discontent, and made him satisfied that the position which God had chosen for him, was better than any that he could choose for himself.

Our next story may be called—

CONTENT AND DISCONTENT.

Two boys had new skates given to them in the early part of winter. It was a frosty day, and they hoped there would be ice enough the

next morning, for them to use their skates on the pond, near their home.

But when they arose the next day, it was raining, and the ice was melting. Neither of them was pleased at the disappointment. The names of the two brothers were Alfred and Peter.

The elder of them, Alfred, said: "Never mind Pete, it's no use to fret and cry. Let's sit down before this blazing fire, and enjoy ourselves over a book."

He then took a nice book from the shelf and sat down cosily in a big arm chair, and soon forgot his disappointment in the pleasure found in his book.

His brother Peter, however, would not follow his example. In a cross tone of voice he said —"A fig for your nice book! I've enough to do with books at school! I want to skate to-day. It's too bad that it should rain so."

Then he posted himself opposite to the window, with his hands in the pockets of his pantaloons, and a face as sour as vinegar. He appeared to be making faces at the rain. Poor fellow! he spent a very unhappy day. There he stood, a discontented boy; and his discontent took away all his comfort. But his brother Alfred had learned to practice the Bible warning against discontent, and we see how much it added to his comfort. Our next story may be called—

MAKE YOUR OWN SUNSHINE.

"Oh, dear, it always does rain when I want to go anywhere!" cried little Jennie Moore. "It's too bad! Now I've got to stay in-doors, and I know I shall have a wretched day of it."

"Perhaps so," said her Uncle Jack; "but you needn't have a wretched day unless you choose."

"How can I help it?" asked Jennie. "I wanted to go to the park, and play on the grass, and pull wild flowers; but now there's not going to be any sunshine at all, and I shall have to stand here and see it rain all the day."

"Well, let's make a little sunshine," said uncle Jack.

"Make sunshine!" said Jennie; "why how you do talk!" And she smiled through her tears. "You haven't got a sunshine factory, have you?"

"Well, I'm going to start one right off, if you'll be my partner," said Uncle Jack.

"And now, let me give you the rules for making sunshine.

"First, Don't think of what you might have been, if the day had been better.

"Second, See how many things are left you to enjoy.

"And Third, Do all you can to make other people happy."

"Well, I'll try the last of the rules first," said Jennie, as she went to work to amuse her little brother Willie, who was crying. By the time she had him riding a chair, and laughing, she was laughing too.

"Well," said Uncle Jack, "I see you are a good sunshine maker, for you've got about all that you and Willie can use just now."

After this she found many a pleasant amusement, and when bed-time came, she kissed her uncle goodnight, and felt sure that she had really been more happy, than if she had spent the day in the park, playing on the grass, and gathering wild flowers. She dreamed that night that her uncle Jack had built a great house, and put a sign over the door, which read thus—

Sunshine Factory.
Uncle Jack and Little Jennie.

She made her uncle laugh, when she told him about her dream the next morning; but she never forgot what we should all remember —that a cheerful heart makes its own sunshine.

Here is a short story about a good bishop, who had learned to mind this warning about discontent, and the comfort which it gave him. We may call it—

THE CONTENTED BISHOP.

This good man had passed through many great trials; but he was never heard to complain, in passing through them. He was always contented and cheerful. An intimate friend of his, who had often admired his calm, happy temper, and who felt as if he would like very much to imitate his example, asked him one day, if he would tell him the secret of the quiet, contented spirit which he always had.

"Yes," said the bishop, "I will gladly tell

you my secret. It consists in nothing more than making a right use of my eyes."

"Please tell me what you mean by this."

"Certainly," said the bishop, "I mean just this. When I meet with any trial, I first of all look up to heaven, and remember that my chief business in life is to get there. Then I look down upon the earth, and think how small a space I shall need in it when I die, and come to be buried; and then I look round in the world, and think how many people there are, who have more cause to be unhappy than I have. And in this way I learn the Bible lesson—"Be content with such things as ye have."

I will close this part of our subject by quoting some appropriate lines, which are called—

SMILE WHENEVER YOU CAN.

"When things don't go to suit you,
    And the world seems upside down,
Don't waste your time in fretting,
    But drive away that frown;
Since life is oft perplexing,
    'Tis much the wisest plan,
To bear all trials bravely,
    And smile whenever you can.

>   And though you are strong and sturdy,
>   You may have an empty purse;
>   But earth has many trials,
>   Which certainly are worse;
>   Yet whether joy or sorrow,
>   Fill up your mortal span,
>   'Twill make your pathway brighter
>   To smile whenever you can."

And so, the first reason why we ought to mind this warning is—for our own comfort.

The second reason why we ought to mind this, is—FOR THE COMFORT OF OTHERS.

The apostle Paul teaches us, that our duty as Christians is—"not to please ourselves, but to please our neighbors, for their good to edification." Rom. xv. 1, 2. This means that we are to try and please those about us, not by doing anything that is wrong, but by setting them a good example, and helping them on in the way to heaven. But there is no better way in which we can do this, than by first learning the lesson of contentment ourselves, and then by our example, helping others to learn it too.

Suppose that you sit down some afternoon, to study your school lesson for the next morning. Outside of the house, under the window of the room in which you are studying, a cross, ill-natured dog is sitting. He is yelling and howling, and barking all the time. Would that be any help, or comfort, to you in studying your lesson? Not at all. On the contrary it would be such a trouble and discomfort to you, that you would be ready to shut up your book, and say,—"Well, I must drive away that noisy dog, or I never can learn my lesson."

And then suppose that there was a tree near the window of the room in which you were studying, and suppose that a little bird should perch himself on one of the branches of the tree, and should warble forth his sweet songs; what a comfort that would be to you! You would feel that the little fellow was a real help to you in learning your lessons. Now, if we give way to an ugly discontented spirit, then, like the barking dog, under the window, we shall only be a plague and a trial to those about us. But, if we learn the lesson of contentment, and have a quiet, gentle spirit, then like the singing bird, we shall be real comforts to our friends, and they will be always glad to have us near them.

Now let us look at some illustrations of this part of our subject. The first may be called—

HOW TO BE BEAUTIFUL.

We cannot all have really beautiful faces, but we can all have sweet pleasant tempers; and a sweet temper gives a loveliness to the face, which is more pleasing than any amount of mere outward beauty. If we only have a smile, and a kind word for every one, we shall be more loved by our friends, and be a greater comfort to them, than if we had the most beautiful faces that were ever seen. A contented spirit, or a sweet temper, is to a home, what sunshine is to the trees of the field, or to the flowers of the garden.

Our next illustration may be called—

LOOKING AT THE BRIGHT SIDE—OR THE FABLE OF THE BUCKETS.

"How dismal you look," said a bucket to his companion, as they were being lowered down into the well together. "Ah," said the other bucket, "I was just thinking how useless it is for us to be filled with water; for no matter how full we may be when we go up, we are always sure to come back empty."

"Why dear me," said the other bucket, "how strange it is to look at it, in that way! Now, I like to look at it differently. I say to myself, no matter how empty we may be when we come to the well, we are sure always to go away full. This is looking at it from the bright side. Try to look at it in this way, and you will be as contented and cheerful as I am."

Let us notice next—

JOHN WESLEY'S CONTENTED SPIRIT.

This excellent man—the founder of the Methodist Church, used to say,—" I dare no more fret, than curse or swear." A friend of his, who was intimately connected with him, for a large portion of his life, in speaking of him after his death, said—" I never saw him fretful, or discontented under any of his trials. And to be in the company of persons of this spirit, always occasioned him great discomfort, and trouble. He said one day—'To have persons around me, murmuring and fretting at everything that happens, *is like tearing the flesh from my bones.* I know that God sits upon His throne, ruling all things. With this thought in my mind, and the grace of God in my heart, I may well learn—'To be content with such things as I have.'" Good Mr. Wesley was minding the Bible warning against discontent, when he used these words, and was setting a good example for us all to follow. What a blessed thing it would be, if all Christians would try to follow his example.

Our next story may be called—

NOT LETTING THE HEART DOWN.

A Christian lady, who spent a good part of her time in visiting the poor and the sick in her neighborhood, went one day to see a poor widow woman, whom she knew very well.

This widow had been trying hard to support herself and her family, by washing and ironing. But her friend, the visitor, had just heard a sad report of her condition. Her health had failed, and she had been obliged to give up her work, and go to bed. The children had nothing to depend upon but her wages, so that her present condition was a hard and trying one. "As I went to her, under these circumstances," says this

Christian lady, "I expected to hear a sad story from her, and to find her looking very gloomy and discontented. But to my surprise she was quite cheerful. She said, in a pleasant way, "I hope soon to be able to go to work again. The people that I work for are willing to wait until I am better; my feet are not quite so bad as they were, and if they only get so that I can stand, I can go on with my ironing. The Doctor says he wont charge anything for his visits, and Jennie my oldest child can do what little cooking we need; so you see, ma'am, I'm pretty well off."

"I was astonished," said this lady, "to find her speaking so cheerfully, when I knew how many things she had to trouble her. I asked her how she could manage to keep up her courage, and be so cheerful, with so much that was sad about her?

"I always find comfort," she said, "in the precious promises of God's word; and then you know,—*there's no use in letting the heart down.*"

"I was amazed," said her visitor, "to hear her speak in this way. Her words had a wonderful effect on me. They went right straight to my heart. I think I never heard a sermon in my life, that did me more good, than that one sentence of this poor woman;—'*there's no use in letting the heart down.*' I was in a good deal of trouble myself at that time, and was letting my heart down. But this widow's words helped and comforted me more than I can tell. I have never forgotten the lesson taught me that day." Now that poor widow woman had learned, and was practising, the Bible warning against discontent. And here we see how learning this lesson brought comfort to herself, and made her a comfort to others.

I have one other story for this part of our subject. We may call it—

CONTENTED TOM.

Tom Flossofer, says a German teacher, was the most cheerful and contented boy I ever knew. I don't think he ever cried; at least I never saw him cry. One day, when his sister Fleda found that her tulips in the garden had been rooted up, by her pet puppy, she cried, as little girls generally do. Just then Tom came round the

THE WARNING AGAINST DISCONTENT. 301

corner whistling. He knew what was the matter, and said—

"What's the use of crying, Fleda? Let's try to put them right." Then he picked up the flowers, and put their roots into the ground again, whistling merrily all the time. He made the bed look smooth and nice, and then took Fleda off to hunt hens' nests in the barn. And he had just the same pleasant way of meeting his own troubles. I saw him flying his big kite one day. While I was looking at him, the string of the kite snapped; and the kite flew away far out of sight. Tom stood still for a moment, looking at it; then he turned round to go home, whistling merrily as he went.

"Why, Tom," said the teacher,—"aren't you sorry to lose that kite?"

"To be sure I am. But what's the use of worrying? That wont bring the kite back again. No, I'm going home to make another."

And it was just the same with him when he broke his leg, and had to be confined to bed.

"Poor Tom," said his sister, as she stood beside his bed and began to cry.

"But I am not poor, though. So you can cry

for me; and then I wont have to do it for myself; and think what a splendid time I shall have to whistle. Besides, when I get well, I shall beat every boy in school on the multiplication table; for I shall say it over and over again, till it makes me sleepy, every time my leg aches."

Now Tom Flossofer had learned the Bible warning against discontent, and we see that it was a comfort to himself, and a comfort to others. These are the first two reasons why we should mind this warning.

The third reason why we should mind this warning is—TO PLEASE GOD.

No trials can ever come upon us in this world, without God's knowledge, and consent. He is so wise, that he never makes a mistake about our trials, and He is so good, that He never lets any trouble come upon us, but what He knows will be for the best.

And when we try to be patient and contented under our trials, because we know that God orders, or permits them, this will be pleasing to Him.

We have some good illustrations of this part of our subject in the Bible.

There is one in the case of the patriarch Job. Perhaps there never was any one in the history of our world, who had so heavy a burden of trials to bear as he had.

He lost his six children, all at once. He was the richest man in the East, where he lived. But all his property was suddenly swept away from him, and he was left in utter poverty. Then he was smitten with a terrible disease, which broke out in painful boils, all over his body, from head to foot.

How hard this must have been for him to bear! Did he fret and worry about it?

No; the first words that he uttered, after all this trouble had come upon him, were these—

"The Lord gave, and the Lord hath taken away; blessed be the name of the Lord."

And some time after this, when one of his friends was speaking as if it were doubtful whether God really loved him, he showed how strong his confidence in God was, by saying—"Though He slay me, yet will I trust in Him." How pleasing this must have been to God!

And then there is David. He had a little child that was very ill, and not expected to live.

He was so anxious for the child's life, that he would not eat anything, but spent his time in fasting, and weeping, and praying for it.

But after awhile, on inquiring about the child, he found that it was dead. Then he wiped away his tears, washed his face—called for something to eat, and went into the temple, to worship God. His servants expressed their surprise, at the strange way in which the king had acted. He told them that they need not be surprised. While the child was yet alive, he said, that he fasted and prayed, because he thought that perhaps it might please God to spare its life. But seeing it was the will of God that the child should not live, there was nothing for him to do, but to be content, and satisfied with His will. David had learned the Bible warning against discontent. And the submissive and contented way in which he acted on that occasion, must have been very pleasing to God.

But the best illustration that we have on this subject, is found in the example of our Blessed Saviour Himself.

When speaking to His disciples one day, about His Father, He said:—" I do always those things that please Him." John viii. 29. This has reference to the work which He did while on earth, and we know that while He was going on with that work, on several occasions the voice of His Father was heard speaking aloud from heaven, and saying—"This is my beloved Son, in whom I am well pleased."

And then, when the time of His suffering and death came, see how He acted. There He is in the garden of Gethsemane. His agony is so great, that He falls to the earth, and His sweat rolls off from Him in great drops of blood. He knows that the scenes of the crucifixion are just before Him, and the terrible sufferings He would have to pass through in bearing the punishment of our sins. And comparing those sufferings to a cup full of bitterness, held out for Him to drink, He prayed thus:—"Father, if it be possible, let this cup pass from me."

But immediately after, He offered this other prayer—" Father, if this cup may not pass from me, except I drink it—Thy will be done!" How beautiful that was! Ah! there was a lesson of submission to the will of God, and of contentment with it, which must have pleased God, more than anything else that ever happened in the history of our world, or of all other worlds put together.

We will close our sermon with one other illustration outside of the Bible. We may call it—

SATISFIED WITH THE BEST.

" I was going down town, in a Fourth Avenue car, one day," says a New York merchant, "when I heard somebody cry out, " Holloa, Mr. Conductor, please stop your car a moment; I can't run very fast." The car stopped, and presently there hobbled into it a little lame boy, about ten or twelve years old. I saw from the nice clothes he wore, that he was the son of wealthy parents; but oh! his face told such a tale of silent suffering! and yet, he was bright and cheerful. He put his little crutch behind him, and placing his poor withered limb in a more easy position, he began to look round at his fellow passengers. A happy smile played over his pale face, and he seemed to take notice of everything. Presently I got a seat next to him, and as he looked around him, I heard him hum-

ming in a low tone, the words of the hymn—
"Hark, I hear an angel sing."

Then I had a little talk with him, and found that he knew and loved the Saviour, and it was *this* which made him so contented and cheerful. He told me he was born with this withered limb, and that the doctor said it never would be any better.

"Well, my dear boy," I said, "under these circumstances, how can you be so happy and cheerful?" His reply was, "Jesus, my Saviour, has sent this trial for me to bear. Father tells me He would not have sent it, unless He knew it would be best for me. And don't you think sir, that I ought to be satisfied with the best?" This touched my heart, and brought tears to my eyes. I was just going to get out of the car then. So I shook hands with the little fellow, and thanked him, for the lesson he had taught me, which I told him I should never forget as long as I lived."

Now this little boy had learned and was practising, the Bible warning against discontent. And we see how well his example illustrates each of the three reasons for minding this warning, of which we have been speaking. *It brought comfort to himself—it gave comfort to others—and was pleasing to God.*

And now, where is our text to-day? Hebrews xiii. 5. What are the words of our text? "Be content with such things as ye have." What is the sermon about? The Bible Warning against Discontent. How many reasons did we have for minding this warning? *Three.* We ought to mind it first—for what?

For our own comfort. Secondly—for what?

For the comfort of others. Thirdly—for what?

To please God.

If we wish to learn this lesson well, we should pray God, in the language of one of our beautiful Collects, "That we may both perceive and **know**, what things we ought to do, and also may **have grace** and power faithfully to perform the **same**, through Jesus Christ our Lord."

XIII.

THE WARNING AGAINST DISOBEYING OUR PARENTS.

"*Honor thy father and thy mother.*"
EXODUS xx. 12.

THESE words take us to Mount Sinai, in Arabia. The children of Israel are encamped around the base of that mountain. Moses has gone up to the top of the mount. The dark clouds which have gathered round the summit of the mountain, hide him from the sight of the people. The mountain is trembling, and shaking like a leaf. The lightning is flashing out from those dark clouds. God has come down upon the top of that mountain, and in a voice of thunder, is giving His ten commandments, which He desired the Israelites, and all other people in the world to mind. The first four commandments, referring to our duty to God, have been delivered. After these come the last six. The first of these, is the fifth commandment, which we have before us in the words of our text. "Honor thy father and thy mother." These ten commandments, are all very important ; but this one, is perhaps the most important of them all. If while we are children, we break this commandment, it will bring more trouble to ourselves, to our parents, and to all about us, than we can bring in any other way. And if we learn to keep this commandment, there is no telling how much good it will secure to ourselves, and to others.

When the apostle Paul refers to this commandment, he says, "it is the first commandment with promise." Indeed it is the only one of the ten commandments which has any promise connected with it. If we learn to keep it, God says—"it shall be well with us, and we shall live long on the earth." This shows us how much God is interested in our keeping this commandment. We may regard the words of our text as giving us—*The Bible Warning against disobeying our parents*. This is the subject of our present sermon.

And there are *three* good things, which minding this warning will bring to us. These should be our reasons for minding it.

*The first good thing which minding this warning will bring to us—is—*HONOR.

We have a good illustration of this in the case of Joseph, whose history is given in the Bible. When his father Jacob commanded him to leave their pleasant home in the vale of Hebron, and go and find out how his brethren were, he obeyed at once. They were feeding their flocks in Shechem. This was a long journey to take in those days. Joseph knew very well how his brethren hated him, because his father loved him more than he did them. On this account he must have known that his visit would not be a pleasant one to him. He was then about seventeen years of age. Now many a boy under these circumstances, would not have been willing to obey his father. But it was different with Joseph. He had learned to mind this warning against disobeying his father. So he went straight forward, and did what his father had told him to do. This brought him into a great deal of trouble at first. His brethren treated him very unkindly. They stripped him of his robe of many colors. They cast him into a pit, and sold him as a slave to be taken down to Egypt. There he was kept in prison for several years. And yet—obeying his father about visiting his brethren, was the best thing that Joseph ever did. It was *this*, which led to his becoming the governor of all the land of Egypt. As Pharaoh sat upon his throne, Joseph stood the next to him in honor and greatness. He was one of the greatest men in the world at that time. But if he had not learned to obey his father, and to mind the warning we are now considering, he never would have gained this honor.

We have another illustration of this part of our subject, in the history of one of our own countrymen—the great and good George Washington.

When he was a boy, he had a great desire to go to sea. A friend of his, who was an officer in the navy, had obtained for him a midshipman's commission. His mother had at first given her consent to his taking this step. But afterwards she changed her mind, and was unwilling to have him go. Yet the preparation for his going went on. The trunk containing his clothes had been packed and taken on board the vessel. Then George went in to say—"good bye"—to his mother. But as he threw his arms round her neck to give her the farewell kiss, she burst into tears, and said she could never have a moment's happiness while he was away from her. "Then, mother dear, wipe away your tears, for I wont go," were George's noble words. Then he had his trunk brought back from the ship, and gave up the idea of going to sea, although he had set his heart upon it. Thus he honored his mother, by obeying not her words only, but her wishes, and altering his whole plan of life, to please her. And this became the turning point in the life of Washington. This led to all his after greatness. If he had not learned this Bible warning against dishonoring his parents, his name would never have had the place it now occupies on the page of history, as the great and successful general of the American Revolution, and the first President of the United States. All this honor came to Washington as the result of his obedience to his parents.

I have one other story for this part of our subject. We may call it—

THE OBEDIENT GERMAN BOY.

The incident to which this story refers, took place in Germany, several hundred years ago. One fine day in Spring, a farmer's boy was sitting on a stone, near a ploughed field, minding his father's cattle. In his hand he held a stout stick, and his good dog Max lay at his feet.

The field before him had just been sowed with grain, and his father had told him to keep a careful watch over it. This boy's name was Herman Billings. As he was sitting there on the stone, he saw a party of knights on horseback coming near. They were finely dressed, and Herman admired their appearance very much. One of them in particular, had a very noble look, and seemed to take the lead of the party.

"Let us go to that house," said this man, pointing to the home of Herman's father.

The nearest approach to the house was over the ploughed field, and as he spoke, the noble rider turned his horse in that direction, and the knights who were with him did the same.

AGAINST DISOBEYING OUR PARENTS.

But Herman sprang up before him, while Max, the good dog, stood by to help if necessary. "Your way lies there, sir," said Herman, grasping his stick, and pointing to a travelled road. "My father told me not to let any one cross this field. I must obey my father, sir. The field has just been sowed and it would injure it very much, if you should ride over it."

" And pray who are you, that would teach us manners, and lay down the law for us ? " said the leader of the knights.

" I am Herman Billings," replied the boy. " My father told me to stay here, and see that no one went over the ploughed field. No one must cross it ;—no, not even the emperor."

Then the noble rider rose proudly in his saddle, looked sternly at the boy, and said—" I am the emperor, now speaking to you, rash boy. Make room for me to go across that field."

" I can well believe that you are the emperor," said the boy, " for you look like him. But no, that cannot be. For the good Emperor Otto, would never try to make a boy disobey his father. He always tries to do what is right ; but it is not right to trample down the field which a poor farmer has just ploughed and sowed."

Two or three of the knights then sprung forward to seize the bold boy, and punish him for speaking so to the emperor: but he cried out,— "Stop there! Don't touch the boy."

Then quietly turning his horse away from the ploughed field, the emperor took the travelled road: and the rest followed him to the house of Herman's father.

After awhile, when Herman went home, he found the emperor and his friends seated round the table, getting some refreshments. As soon as the emperor saw him enter the room, he rose and took him by the hand, and turning to his father, said : " Billings, I want you to send your son to me. A boy who is so obedient to his father, and stands up so nobly for what is right, has the elements of a good character in him, and will make a great man."

So Herman was sent to the emperor's palace. He sent him to school, and had him well educated. Then he entered the army, and rose from one position to another, till he became the most famous general of that day: and finally he wore the crown of Saxony, of which he was appointed the Grand Duke. And all this honor came to him as a reward for the way in which he had learned to obey his parents.

And so we see that we ought to mind this warning, in the first place, because of the honor it will bring to us.

But the second good thing, which minding this warning will bring to us, is—PLEASURE. *And for this we ought to mind it.*

Solomon tells us that religion's ways are—" ways of pleasantness." The ways in which religion lead us, are the ways of keeping God's commandments. David tells us that " in keeping these commandments there is great reward." This " great reward," refers not only to the joy and happiness which God's people will find laid up for them in heaven, as the result of their having kept His commandments; but it also refers to the pleasure which keeping God's commandments will bring to them in this life. And there is not one of God's commandments that will secure to us more pleasure than this we are now considering—the fifth commandment, about honoring and obeying our parents. Let us look at some illustrations of the pleasure which comes to those who learn to mind the Bible warning against disobeying their parents.

Our first illustration may be called—

THE OLD DOCTOR'S STORY.

"I have a little story to tell you, boys," the old doctor said to the children, the other evening.

"One day, when I was a boy, I met my father, on the road to town.

"'Jim,' he said, in a hesitating way, 'I wish you would take this package into the village for me.'

"I was then about twelve years old, and not very fond of work. I had just come from the hayfield, where I had been hard at work since daybreak. I was tired, and dusty, and hungry. It was a two miles' walk into town. I wanted to go home and get my supper, and then wash and dress myself, and go to the evening singing school.

"My first impulse was to refuse to go, for I was vexed to be asked do this after my long day's work. If I had refused, he would have gone himself. He was a gentle, loving, kind old man. Something stopped me from doing what I was just on the point of doing. I have no doubt it was one of God's good angels.

"'Of course, father, I'll take it,' I said heartily, giving my scythe to one of the men. He gave me the package, saying as he did so—'Thank you, Jim, I was going myself, but somehow I don't feel very strong to-day.' He walked with me to the road that turned off towards the town, and as I left him, he laid his hand on my shoulder, saying again—'Thank you, my son. You have always been a good boy to me, Jim.'

"I hurried to town, and back home again. As I came near the house, I saw a great crowd of farm hands about the door. One of them came to me, and with the tears rolling down his face, said—'Your father fell down dead just as he reached the door of his home. The last words he spoke were those he said to you in parting.'

"I am an old man now," said the doctor, who told this story, "but I have thanked God, over and over again, for the help He gave me in honoring and obeying my father on that occasion.

Nothing in the world has ever given me hàlf so much pleasure, as I have found in thinking of my father's last words—' Jim, you have always been a good boy to me.' "

Our next story is one of an opposite character. It shows the pain and sorrow which come from not learning to honor and obey our parents. This story was told by the late Rev. Dr. John Todd, of Pittsfield, Mass., and occurred in his own experience.

And before going on to tell this story, let me say a few words, in order to show how much I am indebted to this good man.

When I was going through the University of Pennsylvania, a young man of 18 or 19 years of age, I was a member of St. John's Church, in the northern part of this city, of which the Rev. Dr. George Boyd was the rector. They were so short-handed for workers in the Church that they made me, youth as I was, the superintendent of their Sunday School. The school had two sessions a day, and the superintendent was expected to occupy the principal part of the second session, in talking to the children. I was frightened when I found this out, and wondered what I should do. But just at that time, I happened to meet with a volume of "Lectures for Children," which had been written and published by Dr. Todd. I felt then as if I had found a gold mine. I used to take a little piece of one of those lectures, and make it the subject of my afternoon's talk. That volume lasted me all through college, and taught me how to talk to children.

And now, for Dr. Todd's illustration of the sorrow and trouble that come from not minding the Bible warning against disobeying our parents.

"When I was a little boy," says the Doctor, "my father was very ill. One day he sent me to the apothecary's to get a particular kind of medicine. I did not want to go. Before getting half way to the apothecary's, I stopped, and made up my mind to go back, and tell a lie about it. So I went home and told my father that the apothecary had none of that medicine left. My father was near his end then. He said to me—' My dear boy, I am suffering very much for want of that medicine.' That made me feel very badly. Then I slipped quietly out, went to the apothecary's, and got some of that medicine. But when I came back it was too late. My father was dying. He had only time to say to me—'Love God, Johnny, and always speak the truth. Now kiss me once more—farewell.'

"In all my after life," said Dr. Todd, "I never was able to forget that act of disobedience to my dying father, and that falsehood told to him. I have repented bitterly of that sin, and believe that God has forgiven it. But the sorrow and trouble occasioned by it, have followed me all the days of my life."

That is a good reason why we should mind the warning against disobeying, and dishonoring our parents.

There is one other illustration of this part of our subject. We may call it—

LITTLE WILLIE'S PLEASURE IN MINDING HIS MOTHER.

Willie Burton was a little boy about eight years old. His mother was an earnest Christian. She had taught him to honor and obey his parents. Whatever his mother told him to do, became the rule and law of Willie's life, and wherever he might be, he never forgot it. And the incident I am now about to tell, shows us how faithful Willie was in carrying out his mother's teaching, and the pleasure he found in doing so.

Willie was taking a short journey in the railway car one day, with his Aunt Matilda. She was a nice lady, but not a Christian. While they were sitting in a beautiful parlor car, waiting for the train to start, a poorly dressed woman, who had a very sad and weary look about her, came in with three little children, one of which was a baby in her arms. A pleasant expression passed over her face, as she sat down in one of the nice easy chairs, and looked around her.

But while she was doing this, the conductor came in, and in a very rough, unkind way, said—"This is not the place for you. You must go into the next car." Some of the passengers smiled, as they saw the frightened mother, and her little ones hurried out to one of the common cars. But in little Willie's face there was a look of pity for them, which made the others feel ashamed.

Soon after they had gone out, Willie said—"Auntie, I'm going to carry my basket of fruit and this box of sandwiches, to that poor woman and her little children in the next car, if you have no objections."

"Don't be foolish, Willie dear," said his Auntie, "you may need them yourself; and then you don't know that she is worthy."

"No, I'll not need them," said Willie, in a low but decided tone. "You know I had a hearty breakfast, before leaving home, and I shan't need a lunch. The poor woman looked so hungry, and tired too, and so did the children. I'll be back in a minute or two. Mother always tells me to do what I can to help the poor and needy. I'm sure if she were here, she would tell me to go."

As Willie went out, his aunt wiped away a tear from her eye, and said, "How like his mother the dear boy is."

A little while after this the train stopped, and Willie and his aunt got out. In doing this, they had to pass through the car where the poor woman and her children were. There they saw a pretty sight. The poor family were feasting as they had perhaps never done before. They were eating the nice sandwiches, and the fruit basket stood open near them. As Willie and his aunt were passing by, they heard the eldest child, with her mouth full of bread and butter, say, as she pointed to Willie—" Mamma, is that pretty boy an angel?" "No," answered the mother, as a grateful look brightened up her faded eyes—"but he is doing an angel's work, bless his dear heart."

Now, it was Willie's desire to honor and obey his mother, which made him so anxious to help and comfort that poor woman and her little ones. And in acting thus, he had the pleasure of knowing that he was really doing an angel's work. And better than that he was doing the work of the Lord of the angels. For when Jesus was on earth, "He went about doing good;" and Willie was "treading in the blessed steps of His most holy life," as he obeyed his mother by trying to help and comfort those needy and suffering ones. And so we see, that the second good thing which minding this warning will bring to us is—pleasure—and this is a good reason for minding it.

*And then the third good thing which minding this warning will bring to us is—*PROFIT*—and for this we ought to mind it.*

God says—"Them that honor me I will honor."

And "the honor which cometh from God' is the most profitable thing we can ever get. We honor God when we keep His commandments, and mind the warning He gives us against disobeying our parents.

We have a good illustration of this part of our subject in the case of David. Several of his older brothers were soldiers in the army of Saul, the king of Israel. Now many a boy, if he had brothers who were soldiers, when the army to which they belonged was marching about the country, or was encamped not far from where he lived, would have been unwilling to stay at home. He would have wanted to go and see the soldiers as they were marching, or drilling, or getting ready for battle. No doubt David felt just as other boys would have done. But he did not give way to this feeling. His father had told him to stay at home, and mind the sheep, and he obeyed his father. He was a brave boy and had all the elements of a soldier in him. When a lion or a bear came and stole one of his lambs, he went boldly out and fought it. And yet, we never once hear of David running away to see the soldiers, or to follow the army. His father's command was in the way of his doing so; and he had learned the warning against disobeying his parents. And what was the result of it? Did it bring any profit to David? Let us see.

One day, his father told him to go to the army, and inquire how his brethren were. He went. And while he was staying there, Goliah, the great giant of the Philistines, came stalking forth in his shining armor. He challenged any soldier in Saul's army to come out and fight him. But they were all afraid. Not one among them would venture to do it. Then David, the shepherd boy, without a sword, or armor, and with nothing in his hand but a sling and a stone, went against the giant, and fought him, and slew him. This secured a great victory to the army of Israel. For the Philistines fled, when they saw their champion, the great giant, fall.

But David would never have gained that victory over the giant of the Philistines, if he had not first gotten the victory over himself, by learning faithfully to honor and obey his parents. Then he became a soldier in Saul's army, then an officer, who was successful in every battle, and finally he was made king of Israel. And the throne which he occupied, the crown which he wore, and the sceptre which he swayed, all helped to make up the profit which came to him for honoring and obeying his parents.

Here is another illustration. We may call it—

WHAT CAME TO A BOY FOR MINDING HIS MOTHER.

The boy told this story to a friend when he was getting to be an old man.

"When I was sixteen years old," said he, "I made up my mind to go to sea. My mother had given her consent. The time for parting came. I stood at our garden gate, on the side of one of the green hills of Vermont. Mother was holding my right hand clasped in hers. While doing so she said—"Edward, my dear boy, I have never seen the ocean; but they tell me that the great temptation of a sailor's life is to drink. Now promise me here, in the sight of God, and before letting go your mother's hand, that you will never drink intoxicating liquor." I gave her the promise which she asked for, which has been faithfully kept.

Since then I have gone round the world. I have visited England — Europe — India — China — Japan — San Francisco — the Mediterranean, the Cape of Good Hope, the Arctic, and the Antartic circle. And during the forty years I have been following the sea, I have never looked at a glass sparkling with liquor, when my mother's form, by the garden gate of our Vermont home, did not rise up before me. I have thought of the command that she gave me about drinking; and I have thanked God, over and over again, for helping me to honor my mother by obeying her."

"And now tell me," said the old sailor's friend, "what has been the result of it?"

"The result was," said the sailor, "that I was for years, one of the most successful captains that ever sailed from the port of Boston. And now I have retired from active service, and have a fortune sufficient to support myself and family comfortably during the evening of my days." And here we see the profit which came to that good sailor, for his faithfulness in honoring his mother by keeping her command.

I have just one other story. We may call it—

THE PROFIT OF OBEDIENCE AND KINDNESS.

This story refers to what happened to a family in Germany some years ago. The parents of this family were good Christian people, but they were very poor. They had ten children, who had been faithfully taught to honor and obey their parents, and to be kind to all who are in trouble A poor widow woman, who was a neighbor of theirs, had just died, leaving a little daughter named Gretchen, with no money to support her, and no relatives in the world with whom she could live. One evening, about sunset, Gretchen came round to the door of the good German mother's house, and asked if she could have a home with them.

"I don't know how we can make out," said the mother, "and yet we cannot let you starve, poor child."

Just then a stranger was passing by. He had heard the child's question to the mother, and her reply, and felt interested in the matter. He asked if he could have some supper with the family, and was invited in. He found out by inquiry, all the particulars about little Gretchen, and then said—"Can't you manage to keep her? I suppose you have none of your own?"

The mother smiled at this, and said—"O, we have only ten, sir."

Then the call was made for supper, and the little ones all came trooping in. The stranger watched them with great interest. Their faces were all clean; their hair neatly brushed, and their patched and worn clothes looked as though they had taken the greatest possible care of them. He was engaged in conversation with the parents of the family, and yet he kept a careful eye on the children. He was delighted to notice, how instantly they minded every word that was spoken to them by their father or mother, and how ready they all were to share whatever they had, with poor little Gretchen. Then he said, "good-bye" to them, and went away.

The next day a soldier, in grand military dress, rode up on horseback, and called for the mother. When she opened the door he gave her a large letter, with the seal of the emperor of Germany upon it. She trembled as she broke the seal, and opened the letter. And what do you suppose that the letter said? Why, it said that the man who had taken supper with them the night before, was the emperor, and that he was so pleased with the ten children, with the way in which they honored and obeyed their parents, and with their kindness to poor Gretchen, that he had decided to make each of them a present of $100, which would be paid to them each year as long as they lived. Only think of that; $1,100 a year because the stranger who took supper with them, was so pleased with their ready obedience to their parents, with their respect to him, and their unselfish kindness to the poor orphan Gretchen. Some of you may think that this sounds like a made-up story. But it is not so. It is a true story. The letter was signed—"Joseph, Emperor of Austria." He was the stranger, who had eaten a potato supper with that poor family, the night before.

And this is a beautiful illustration of the profit that comes from minding the Bible warning against disobeying our parents.

Now where is our text? Exodus xx. 12. What are the words of the text? "Honor thy father and thy mother." What is the sermon about?

The Bible warning against disobeying our parents. How many good things will minding this warning bring to us? Three. What is the first? Honor. What is the second? Pleasure. What is the third? Profit. Honor, pleasure, and profit, will certainly be ours, if we mind this warning. Now let it be our daily, constant prayer, that God may help us to mind it, and then all the blessings promised to those who keep this commandment, will be ours, both in this world, and in the world to come.

"HONOR THY FATHER AND THY MOTHER."

XIV.

THE WARNING AGAINST SWEARING.

"*Swear not.*"—MATT. V. 34.

THESE words were spoken by our blessed Saviour. Here He gives us the substance of the third commandment, put into the very shortest possible form. This is a very important commandment. What God tells us here is:—"Thou shalt not take the name of the Lord thy God in vain: for the Lord will not hold him guiltless that taketh His name in vain." Here, as God gave this third commandment, on the top of mount Sinai, we count up twenty-seven words. But in our text, Jesus reduces all these many words to two. And in these two words we have the Bible warning against swearing. This is the subject of our sermon to-day.

And in handling this subject, I wish to speak of—*three*—good reasons why we ought to mind this warning.

And the first reason why we ought to mind this warning is—BECAUSE SWEARING IS A DISGRACE TO OURSELVES.

The greatest honor that any one can have, is—"the honor that cometh from God." And if you ask how we are to get this honor? God gives us the answer Himself, when He says—"Them that honor me, I will honor." And one of the best ways in which we can honor God, is by showing proper respect to His Holy name. And when we do this, we may be sure that God will honor us.

But when we swear, and take God's Holy Name in vain, we dishonor Him. And then we may be sure that He will dishonor us, or cause disgrace to rest upon us. And we can have no greater disgrace than to know that God is displeased with us; and that the holy angels, and all the good people in heaven, are displeased with us. And yet we may be sure that this is the case when we swear. It is a disgraceful thing to swear.

Here are some illustrations of this part of our subject. Our first story may be called—

WHAT A LITTLE GIRL THOUGHT OF SWEARING.

A Captain in the army, had a month's leave of absence from the camp. He returned home to spend that holiday among the members of his family. While there, he went to make a visit to an uncle who lived in the country, several miles distant from his home.

This uncle had a dear little girl, about ten years old, who loved the Saviour, and was trying to please Him in all things. She sat on her father's knee, while he was talking with his nephew, the captain, and was very much distressed to hear how terribly he swore.

When he was going away, the little girl walked out with him towards the barn, where his horse was waiting for him.

As they were going there, she said to him—"I don't like to hear you swear, cousin John, because swearing is such a disgraceful thing."

"I know it's wrong, my dear," he said, "and I'm sorry I've got into the way of doing it."

In the same gentle way, the little girl said—"Well, then, if you know it is wrong, why do you do it?" Now this was a question much easier for her to ask, than for him to answer. He felt it to be so, and did not attempt to answer it. But in speaking of it afterwards to a friend, he said—"I never felt a reproof in all my life, as I did the one given me by that little girl. I kept asking myself her question, over and over again: 'If I know it's wrong, why do I do it?' And then I made up my mind, that by the help of God, I never would do so again. It is now a number of years since this took place. But from that day to this, I have never sworn another oath."

That brave soldier was led to feel the truthfulness of the lines written by one of our English poets, who says—

> "It chills my blood to hear the great Supreme,
> Lightly appealed to, on each trifling theme.
> Maintain your rank, vulgarity despise:
> To swear is neither brave, polite, nor wise."

Our next story may be called—

THE MINISTER'S REPROOF.

A Lieutenant in the English army had gotten into the habit of swearing fearfully. At one time he was stationed at New Castle, England.

While staying there, he got into a quarrel with some laboring men who were working for him, on one of the public streets. They all got very much excited, and were swearing terribly. Just then, the clergyman of a Scotch Church in the neighborhood, was passing by. He was greatly shocked by the awful oaths which he heard. On looking round at the excited crowd, he saw among them, one man whom he knew. Going up to him, he laid his hand on the man's shoulder, and said—"Oh John, John! what is this I hear? You are only a poor collier boy, and yet swearing at this terrible rate! What will become of you? Did you ever think what a disgraceful thing it is, for you, or any one, to take in vain the holy name of that great God, in whom we live, and move, and have our being?"

And then, turning to the lieutenant, who had been swearing as badly as any of them, he said, "You'll please excuse this poor man, sir, for he is only an ignorant fellow, and does not know any better."

We are not told what effect the minister's words had on poor John.

But the lieutenant felt them deeply. They made him feel very much ashamed of himself. The next day he called on the minister, and thanked him sincerely for the words that he had spoken.

"I never thought before," said he, "what a disgraceful thing it is for poor sinful creatures such as we are, to take in vain the name of the great God of heaven. But I see it now, sir, and I wish to tell you that I have sworn my last oath.'

I have one other story to illustrate this part of our subject. We may call it—

THE BOSTON BOY.

There was a little boy in Boston, about twelve years old. He was quite small for his age, and used to do errands for four gentlemen whose stores were next door to each other.

One day, as he returned from an errand, the gentlemen were talking together in one of their stores, and were using a great many oaths in their conversation. As the little boy stood there, waiting for another order, they began to make fun of him, for his size. One of the gentlemen said to him: "You never can amount to anything, or do much business, because you are so little." The little fellow looked at them awhile and then said—" Well, small as I am, there is one thing that I can do, which none of you big men are able to do." "Ah, indeed," said they. " Well, pray tell us what that is." "Why," said the little fellow—"*I can keep from swearing,* which is a disgraceful thing to do."

The blushes on the faces of those four merchants, told how much ashamed they felt. But they had nothing more to say to that brave little boy.

And so the first reason why we ought to mind this warning against swearing, is because it is a disgrace to ourselves.

And the *second reason why we ought to mind it, is because*—IT IS AN INJURY TO OTHERS.

If we have a companion, who sets us a bad example, by constantly breaking one of God's commandments, he would be doing us a great injury, by tempting us to commit the same sin that he was committing. If a person who had the small-pox, or the scarlet fever, should want to keep company with us, we can understand how much injury he would do us, because we should be likely to catch his disease from him. If a playmate of yours, had the power of taking away from his companions the use of their limbs, and of making them lame; of taking away the use of their eyes, and of making them blind; we can easily understand how much injury such a person would do to his companions. But if we have among our playmates one who is in the habit of swearing, and taking God's holy name in vain, there is no telling how much injury he may do us. By his example, he may lead us to commit the same great sin, that he is committing, and this would be a terrible injury. And we ought to mind this warning against swearing, because of the injury it will lead us to do to others. Here are some incidents to illustrate this part of our subject.

The first may be called—

WHAT A BOY DID.

Willie Jones was a Sunday-school boy, about twelve years of age, and was trying to be a Christian. One summer, his father had promised him that he should spend his vacation in the country. Willie was delighted with this idea, for he was very fond of the country, and expected to have a great deal of pleasure there.

Mr. Jones, his father, made an arrangement with the farmer who supplied them with butter and milk, to have Willie go and board with his family, during vacation time. The farmer's name was Mr. Jenkins. He was an industrious man, and managed his farm very well. The one fault about him was, that he was a great swearer. This grieved and troubled Willie very much. But still he took pleasure in going through the woods, hunting for birds' nests—in watching the milking of the cows—the churning of butter, and all the other work that was carried on about the farm.

One day, during harvest time, he went out to try and help the men in their work.

But while this was going on, he was very much hurt to hear Mr. Jenkins, the owner of the farm, swearing terribly. This made Willie feel very badly. He bore it as long as he could. Then he turned to Mr. Jenkins, and said: "Well, I guess I'll have to go home to-morrow."

" Why Willie," said Mr. Jenkins, who had got

to be very fond of him, " I thought you were going to stay with us all summer."

" So I was," said Willie, " but you see, I can't stand this swearing. It hurts my feelings, and does me a great deal of harm ; so I guess I'll have to go home."

Willie's words had a great effect on the farmer. They made him feel that he was committing a great sin, and injuring all about him, by the habit of swearing.

" Well Willie," said he, " you can stay on, as you intended to do, and I promise you faithfully, that during your stay you shall never hear any more swearing from me." The farmer kept his word, and Willie stayed there, till the close of summer, and had a real good time.

Now boys, here is a good example for you to follow. Learn to mind the Bible warning against swearing, and try to get others to mind it too, as Willie Jones did, and there is no telling how much good you may do.

Our next story may be called :

SWEARING IN HEBREW.

Several years ago, an officer of the navy was a

passenger in one of the cars that runs from Jersey City to Trenton. He was engaged in earnest conversation with a gentleman who sat next to him, and accompanied what he had to say with terrible oaths. A young lady, who was an earnest Christian, was sitting so near him that she had to hear every oath he uttered. At first she tried to bear it patiently; but as the swearing continued, and grew louder and worse, she was very much distressed. She looked round for another seat, further away from the swearer. But every seat in the car was occupied, and it was impossible for her to get away.

Then she made up her mind to try and stop his swearing in some way. After thinking over it for a while, she turned to the officer, and said: "Sir, can you speak in Hebrew?"

He was very much surprised by this question, and after looking around him, in a confused sort of way, he answered the lady's question by saying, "Well, I guess I could, if I tried."

"Sir," said the lady, "it is very painful to me, and the other passengers, to hear the terrible oaths that you have been using. And if you swear any more, it will be a great relief to us if you will please do your swearing in Hebrew."

The officer seemed thoroughly ashamed of himself. His face turned first red, and then white. He looked first at the young lady, and then at the floor of the car, and then out of the window. But he stopped talking ; and not another oath was heard from him, all the rest of the journey, either in English or in Hebrew. Here, we see how that officer was doing a real injury, to all the passengers in that car, by his swearing.

I have only one other story for this part of our subject. We may call it—

THE PIOUS SAILOR AND THE SWEARING MERCHANT.

A merchant and ship owner, in the city of Boston, was standing at the entrance of his warehouse, one day, talking with another gentleman on business. A pious sailor, belonging to one of his vessels, came to the warehouse at that time, to get something for the captain of the ship. But seeing that the merchant who owned the vessel, was standing in the doorway, talking with a friend, the sailor modestly stepped aside, as he did not wish to interrupt the conversation. While waiting there he heard terrible swearing, in which the name of Jesus was profanely used. On turning to look, he found that it was the merchant, who owned the ship in which he sailed, who was the speaker, and who was doing all this swearing. Then he changed his position, and coming in front of the merchant with his head uncovered, and his cap under his arm, he spoke to him, and said:

"Sir, will you excuse me if I speak a word to you?"

The gentleman looked at him for a moment, and recognizing him as one of the crew of his vessel, which had lately returned from sea, and supposing that he might have something to say to him about the business of the ship, told him to speak on.

"You won't be offended, then, sir, with a poor ignorant sailor, if he tells you his feelings, will you, sir?"

"Certainly not," said the merchant, "speak freely, all that you wish to say."

"Well, then, sir," said the sailor, with much feeling, "will you be so kind, as not to take the name of my blessed Jesus in vain? He is a dear good Saviour. 'He took my feet out of the horrible pit, and the miry clay, and established my goings.' O, sir, don't, if you please, take the name of my Master, the Lord Jesus, in vain! He is your Creator, sir, as well as mine. He has made us, and preserves us, and is always doing us good. It almost breaks my heart to hear His Holy name taken in vain."

This was said so respectfully, and yet with so much earnestness and feeling, that the heart of the merchant was quite touched ; and his eyes filled with tears, as he said:

"My good fellow, God helping me, I will never again take the name of the Lord Jesus Christ, the Saviour, in vain."

"Thank you, sir," said the honest sailor; and putting on his tarpaulin cap, he went away to his work.

Here we see, how well this good sailor had learned the Bible warning against swearing. And we see how much pain and injury, the swearing of that merchant had caused him. And this shows us, that the second reason why we ought to mind this warning, is because swearing is an injury to others, as well as a disgrace to ourselves.

But the third reason why we ought to mind this warning, is—BECAUSE SWEARING IS AN OFFENCE TO GOD.

Just think what it is that we are doing to God, when we swear, and take His Holy name in vain. When the Israelites were coming out from Egypt, God met them at Mount Sinai. He came down on the top of that mountain, in the most solemn manner, and gave them in a voice of thunder, His ten commandments. The third of these is the commandment against swearing. But when we swear, it is just as if we should take the leaf out of the Bible, on which this commandment is printed, and should tear it in pieces, and trample it under our feet; and should say, while we were doing this: "We don't care for God's commandments, and we are going to swear as much as we please." What an offence to God that would be! There is something awful in the very thought of it. It would not surprise us, if the lightning from heaven, should blaze forth against the person who did this, and consume him ; or if the ground should cleave asunder beneath him, and swallow him up. Yet this is just what every swearer does. Surely then, there can be no greater offence to God, than that which swearing offers to Him.

Here are some illustrations of this part of our subject. The first may be called—

OUR FATHER.

Johnnie Robins was a little boy, about ten years old. He was trying to be a Christian, and he showed this in all his conduct. He was never heard to speak a bad word. Most of the boys in the school, to which he went, were in the habit of swearing in their play. One day during recess, one of his classmates came up to him and said: "Johnnie, the other boys swear more or less, when they are playing. But I never heard you swear any. Why don't you do it too?" This was Johnnie's answer. "I would sooner cut my tongue out of my mouth, than use it for swearing. God is my Heavenly Father. Do you think I could ever allow myself to speak ugly words to my Father in Heaven?"

That little boy had learned the Bible warning against swearing, because he knew that it would be an offence to God.

Our next story may be called—

HOW LITTLE WILLIE FELT ABOUT SWEARING.

Willie was a little boy about eight years old. His mother was a good Christian woman, and tried, in every way, to make him a Christian too. She had been particularly careful to teach him the Bible warning against lying, and swearing. Willie loved his mother very much, and tried to remember and follow her teaching. He was generally very bright, and happy. But one afternoon, when he came home from school, he looked very sad, and unhappy. His mother said, " Have you hurt yourself, Willie?" " No," was his reply. " Have you been in any mischief?" " No:" he said again. Still she wondered what could be the matter with her boy. At supper time he hardly ate a mouthful, and never spoke a word, though he was always in the habit of talking freely at meal-time. When supper was over, his mother said to him: " Willie, my dear boy, do tell me what is the matter with you?"

"O, mother," he said, " on coming home from school this afternoon,—I swore. It was the first time I ever did it. And the moment I had

THE WARNING AGAINST SWEARING. 351

spoken the oath, and thought of the great offence I had committed against God, I felt frightened, and ran home as fast as I could. I would rather be dumb, all the days of my life, than to be a swearer. Mother dear, wont you please kneel down with me, and ask God to forgive me for taking his name in vain?"

Then they kneeled down together, and his mother asked God to forgive the great sin he had committed, and give him grace never to do so again. When they rose from their knees, Willie wiped away the tears from his face, and said: "Thank you, my dear mother. That was the first time I ever swore, and with the help of God, I am sure it will be the last." And so Willie learned the Bible warning against swearing, from seeing what an offence it was to God.

Our next story may be called—

AFRAID TO SWEAR ALONE.

If persons are going to steal, or do other wrong things, they generally wish to be alone, and to have no one see them. But it is different with swearers. They like to swear in public, and to have many persons hear them. Boys think that it is manly to swear; and men think that it proves they are brave and courageous. And yet it is true, that those who swear the worst, often prove to be the greatest cowards.

A Christian merchant was greatly shocked, one day, by hearing a man who came into his office, swearing in a most horrible manner. He looked at the man for awhile, and then said to him, "My friend, I will give you ten dollars, if you will go into the village church yard, at 12 o'clock to-night, and swear the same oaths there, when you are alone with God, that you have just been swearing here." "Agreed!" said the man. "That's an easy way for making ten dollars."

"Well," said the merchant, "you come here to-morrow, and tell me that you have done so, and you shall have the money."

At midnight, the man started for the grave yard. It was a very dark and dismal night. As he entered the grave yard, not a sound could be heard. All was as still as death. Then the merchant's words,—"All alone with God"—rang in his ears. He felt, as he had never done before, that God was there, close by his side. This thought frightened him. The idea of swearing,

THE WARNING AGAINST SWEARING. 353

in the immediate presence of God, seemed terrible. He did not dare to utter a single oath. Instead of doing this, he ran toward his home. On arriving there, he went to his own chamber, and falling on his knees, offered the prayer, "God be merciful to me a sinner." And from that night, he never uttered another oath. The thought of what an offence it was to God, taught him the Bible warning against swearing.

I have only one other story to illustrate this part of our subject. We may call it—

STRUCK DUMB BY SWEARING.

The incident here referred to, took place some years ago, in the State of Indiana. The person to whom it relates, was named John Lyman.

He had been a sailor for many years, and had learned to swear, in the most terrible manner. On giving up going to sea, he settled in Indiana. Here he had a company of half a dozen men in his employ, who used to go about the country, working under him in different ways. On one occasion, they were employed in moving out all the contents of an old barn, and stowing them away in a new barn, which had just been finished. While this work was going on, something occurred that made Lyman very angry. Then he began to swear at a terrible rate. He kept on swearing worse and worse. It got to be so awful, that the men stopped working, and put their hands to their ears, that they might not hear any more of those dreadful oaths. While this was going on, all at once, Lyman stopped speaking. Then he staggered, and fell to the ground. He had suddenly lost the power of speech. He was unable to move. The men carried him to the farm-house. After awhile he rallied, so as to be able to move about as usual. But from that day to the day of his death, he was never able to speak another word. What an offence his swearing must have been to God, when He punished him for it, in this fearful way!

And now, where is our text to-day? Matt. v. 34. What are the words of the text? Swear not. What is the sermon about? The Bible warning against swearing. How many reasons did we have for minding this warning? Three. What is the first reason why we ought to mind this warning? *Because swearing is a disgrace* to ourselves. What is the second reason? *Because swearing is an injury to others.* What is the third reason? *Because swearing is an offence to God.*

There is a beautiful Collect, in the Communion Service of our Church, which furnishes us with just such a prayer as we ought to offer, if we hope to obtain God's help, in learning to mind this warning against swearing. These are the words of the prayer—"Almighty God, unto whom all hearts are open, all desires known, and from whom no secrets are hid; cleanse the thoughts of our hearts by the inspiration of thy Holy Spirit; that we may perfectly love thee, and worthily magnify thy holy name, through Jesus Christ our Lord. Amen."

XV.

THE WARNING AGAINST SELFISHNESS.

"*We—ought—not to please ourselves.*"
ROMANS XV. 1.

THESE words are only a part of the verse from which they are taken. There are other words in this verse, but they do not suit the subject we are now to consider, and so we leave them out. The words now selected, "We—ought—not to please ourselves," make a very nice text for the subject of our present sermon; which is "The Bible warning against selfishness."

We cannot be true Christians if we give way to selfishness. A real Christian is one who tries to be like Christ. Nobody was further removed from selfishness, than was Jesus, our blessed Saviour. In the next verse to that in which our text is found, the Apostle Paul tells us that—"*Christ pleased not himself.*" When he was born in a stable, and cradled in a manger, He was not pleasing Himself ; when He spent forty days in the wilderness, fasting and being tempted of the devil, he was not pleasing Himself ; when He became a man of sorrows and acquainted with grief, He was not pleasing Himself ; when He was so poor that He could say,—" the foxes have holes, and the birds of the air have nests, but the Son of Man hath not where to lay his head," He was not pleasing Himselt ;—when He went through that awful baptism of blood in the garden of Gethsemane, He was not pleasing Himself; when He was nailed to the cross, and died in awful agony, and was buried, He was not pleasing Himself, but His Father in heaven. And we never can be true Christians, till we learn to follow His example, in this respect, and mind the Bible warning against selfishness.

And if we ask ourselves the question what sort of a thing selfishness is ? we shall find that there are *three* things about it, each of which furnishes a good reason why we should mind the Bible warning against it.

In the first place, selfishness is—an UGLY—*thing.* And this is a good reason why we should mind the warning against it.

One thing that helps to make our bodies look pleasing, or beautiful, is when the different parts, like the head, or the hands, or the feet, are all of a proper size, or shape. But suppose we should see a boy, or a girl, ten or twelve years old, with a head as big as a bushel measure; with feet as large as an elephant's; or with hands ten times as large as they ought to be; should we say that their bodies were beautiful? No, every one who saw them, would say how ugly they were! A body of which the head, or the hands, or the feet are allowed to grow out of their proper size, must always be ugly.

And it is just the same with our souls, when we give way to wrong feelings. This makes one part of the soul become larger than it ought to be. Then its proper shape, or proportion is lost, and this must make the soul ugly, just as it does the body. If we give way to pride, it will have this effect ; and so will anger, and so will selfishness. There is nothing perhaps that makes a person look so ugly and disagreeable, as giving way to selfishness.

Let us look at some illustrations of this part of our subject. Our first story may be called—

THE WARNING AGAINST SELFISHNESS. 359

HOW UGLY SELFISHNESS MADE A LITTLE BOY.

Anne Dawson was a little girl, about eight years old. She was lying in bed, very ill with a fever. In the same room was her brother, two or three years older than herself. He was a selfish boy, and was then busily engaged in making a boat. In doing this, the noise he made was very distressing to his poor sister. She begged him to stop making that noise. But he went on pounding away, and paying no attention at all to his sister. How thoroughly selfish this was!

Presently, in a gentle voice Anne said, "Robbie dear, wont you please get me a glass of cold water? My throat is very dry, and my head aches terribly."

Robbie paid no attention to what his sister said, but went on pounding away at his boat. Pretty soon she begged again, for a glass of cold water. Robbie called out sharply: "Wait awhile, Anne, I am too busy now.' Again his sister pleaded for a drink. Then he hastily poured out some water from a pitcher, which had been standing all day in the sun. "Oh! not that water, brother," said Anne, in a gentle tone, "please bring me some fresh and cool, from the spring."

"Don't bother me so, Anne. You see how busy I am. I'm sure this water is good enough." And then the thoughtless, selfish boy, went on again pounding away on his boat.

"Oh! my head, my poor head! said Anne, as she sipped a little of the warm water, and then lay back on her pillow. That was her last movement. She died that night. The last favor asked of her brother, he had denied her, in the exercise of his selfishness. For thousands of gold and silver I would not have had Robert's feelings, when he stood by the grave of his sister, and thought of all this. He was a thoroughly selfish boy. And when we think of him, as acting out his selfishness, in the chamber of his dying sister, we cannot imagine anything more ugly than this makes him appear.

But sometimes, we can understand a thing better, by looking at it in the way of contrast, and getting an idea how the opposite of it appears. We have seen how ugly selfishness makes those who practice it appear. Now let us look at one or two illustrations of unselfishness, and we shall see how beautiful it makes those who practice it appear. Our first illustration may be called—

THE UNSELFISH MINER BOY.

Some time ago, an accident occurred in a coal mine, in England, by which several lives were lost. Two boys managed to get hold of a chain, that was hanging by the side of a pit; and so they had the hope of being saved, if they could hold on till help came. Very soon a man was lowered down, in the little car attached to the engine, at the entrance of the mine, to see if there were any alive, who could be drawn up. In going down, he first came to a boy, named Daniel Harding. When the man offered to take him up, the noble fellow said: "Don't mind me. I can hold on a little longer; but there is Joe Brown just below here. He is nearly exhausted. Save him first." Joe Brown was saved, and so was his unselfish friend. Daniel Harding was trying to be a Christian, and we see how well he had learned the Bible warning against selfishness. And how beautiful his unselfishness makes him appear!

There is only one other story for this part of our subject; we may call it—

THE UNSELFISH SCHOOL BOY.

His name was Arthur Campbell. He was about nine years old. One Saturday afternoon his mother said to him: "Arthur, my dear boy, do you think you can practice a lesson in self-denial this afternoon, for the good of another person?"

"I don't know mother, but at any rate I can try. What is it you mean?"

"Why, you know, little Susan Gray wants to go to Sunday-school to-morrow. But she can't go in her old ragged clothes; so I am making her a frock, a cape, and a bonnet, in order that she may go. I shall have to work till late this evening, to get them done. This is what I expected to do. But your father has just sent in a long account, to be added up before tea time. If I attend to this account I can't finish the clothes. Now the question is, shall poor Susan go without her clothes for another week, or will my dear boy give up his play this afternoon, and cast up these accounts for me?"

THE WARNING AGAINST SELFISHNESS. 363

Arthur hesitated a moment. Then he ran upstairs to his own little room. He shut the door, and then burst into tears. " What shall I do ?" he said to himself. "I only come home from school on Saturdays, and go back on Mondays. If I give up flying my kite this afternoon, I shall have to wait a whole week, before I can get another chance to fly it. And then it's my new kite, and a real beauty; and this is such a royal breezy day for it ; and so many of the fellows will be out with their kites this afternoon ; and I do so want to show them mine. And yet I know poor little Susan has looked forward to going to Sunday-school to-morrow, and she will be dreadfully disappointed not to go. What shall I do?" Then he kneeled down, and asked God to guide him in this matter, and help him to do what was right. When he rose from his knees, these words of our Saviour came into his mind : "As ye would that men should do to you, even so do to them." This settled the question. Dashing away the tears from his eyes. he put his new kite safely away in the closet, for another week, and going down-stairs to his mother, he said: " Rather than little Susan shall be disappointed, I will give up my kite-flying, mother dear, and will stay home and settle those accounts."

His mother stooped down to kiss him. As she did so, he felt the warm tear-drops from her eyes, fall upon his cheek. They were tears of gladness, to see her dear boy minding the Bible warning against selfishness. And Arthur was much happier that afternoon, than if he had been flying his kite in the fields. But the next day, when he saw little Susan Gray in church, with her new clothes on, and looking as pleased and happy as possible, Arthur felt more real pleasure than all the kites in the country could have given him.

Now, Arthur's noble conduct, resulting from his unselfishness, made him appear really beautiful. But if, instead of this, he had disobeyed his mother, and had spent that afternoon in flying his kite, how ugly his selfishness would have made him appear! And so, the first reason, why we ought to mind this Bible warning against selfishness, is because selfishness is an *ugly* thing.

THE WARNING AGAINST SELFISHNESS.

The second reason why we ought to mind it is—because selfishness is—a DISAGREEABLE THING.

When the things about us, mind the laws which God has made to govern them, then, they are all agreeable. The light of the sun is pleasant to see; the gentle sighing of the wind is pleasant to hear; and the fragrance of the rose, and other flowers, is pleasant for us to smell, just because the sun shines, and the wind blows, and the flowers give out their fragrance, according to the laws which God has made for them. Doing this, makes them all agreeable.

But, if the sun should blaze forth, with light ten times stronger than God has arranged for it to give, this would make our days very disagreeable. And so it would be with the wind, and the flowers, and the other things about us; they would all become disagreeable to us, because they were not minding the laws which God made to govern them. And it is just so with ourselves. God's law for us to mind, is that we are not to seek our own things, but the things of others. In the words of our present text it is—that—"we ought not to please ourselves." If we mind this law, it will make us unselfish, and then we shall always be agreeable to those about us. But if we do not mind this law, then we shall become selfish, and this will make us disagreeable to all who are about us. We shall find out how true it is, that selfishness is a disagreeable thing.

Let us look at some illustrations of this part of our subject. Our first story may be called—

THE EFFECT OF A LITTLE GIRL'S SELFISHNESS.

A Christian lady, who taught in Sunday School, was talking to her class on the evils of selfishness, when she illustrated it by this story, from her own experience. "I remember," she said, "when I was a little girl, I had not learned the Bible warning against selfishness. My Grandma, whom I loved very much, was dangerously ill, and near the end of her life. One day, when I was playing with my doll, in the corner of the room, she asked me to bring her a glass of water. I did not mind her at first, but went on playing with my doll. Then she called me again. After this second call, I went and got the water, and carried it to her. But I did it in a very unkind, and disagreeable way. When she had drunk the water, she said—' Thank you, my dear child,

THE WARNING AGAINST SELFISHNESS. 367

for bringing me the water; but it would have given me so much more pleasure if you had only brought it willingly.' Now it was nothing but my selfishness which led me to act in that way. My dear Grandma died soon after that. She never asked me to do anything for her again. I have never forgotten how disagreeable my selfishness made me appear to my dear dying Grandma. It is forty years ago *to-day*, since this took place; and yet there is a sore spot in my heart, which it left there, and which I must carry with me as long as I live."

And now we may take some illustrations in the way of contrast, showing how agreeable we can make ourselves when we learn to be unselfish. Our first story may be called—

THE WONDERFUL AUNT BESSIE.

Two little girls were nestled together in bed one night, and were talking earnestly to each other, as little ones are apt to do, when they sleep together. They were talking about their Aunt Bessie; and who should come to the door, just then, but Aunt Bessie herself? She was going to her own room, and hearing the children talk, she stopped at the door, as it was a little ajar, to hear what it was all about. "Do you know," said Minnie, the younger one, to her companion, " do you know what it is that makes my Aunt Bessie's forehead so smooth?"

"Why yes," said her friend, and bed-fellow, Mary Lee. "She isn't old enough to have wrinkles. That's as plain as anything."

"Oh! she is, Mary. She's old enough to have a forehead full of wrinkles; but she has a way of keeping 'em off, and I don't see when they'll ever get a chance to come. You see her forehead is smooth because she is *so unselfish, and never frets.*

"You think there's no one in the world like your Aunt Bessie, don't you, Minnie?"

"Well, may be there are people that are just as good, but I don't know where they live, I'm sure. My Aunt Bessie is wonderful about her unselfishness, and about not fretting. I really believe that if the house was on fire she would be just as pleasant as could be about it. She would think about everybody else, but never once about herself. She'd help mother, and the baby, and me out of the house, and then she'd help to get all the things out. Yet she wouldn't worry, or fret, or scold at anybody; but do just as if it was all right, and couldn't be helped; for that's the way she always acts about everything, no matter how bad and unpleasant it is. I always like to hear her read the Bible, for she lives just like the Bible. She's just as sweet, and kind, and unselfish, as it tells us to be. And this is what makes Aunt Bessie so pleasant and agreeable."

Our next story may be called—

A GREAT MAN'S UNSELFISHNESS.

One of the greatest landscape painters that England ever had, was the late Joseph W. Turner. The incident now to be told of him, shows that he was not only great,—but good. He was a member of the committee, whose business it was, to arrange about hanging up the pictures, that were sent in for exhibition to the Royal Academy of London. On one occasion, when the Committee were just finishing their work, and the walls of the Academy were already crowded, Mr. Turner's attention was called to a picture which had been painted by an unknown artist, from some distant part of the country, and who had no friend in the Academy to watch over his interest.

"That is an excellent picture," said Mr. Turner, as soon as his eye rested on it. "It must be hung up somewhere for exhibition."

"That is impossible," said the other members of the committee, with one voice. "There is no room left. The arrangement already made cannot be disturbed. No space can be found for another picture."

"That picture must have a place somewhere," said the generous artist. Then he deliberately took down one of his own pictures, and put the painting of this unknown artist in its place.

How noble that was! Turner had learned thoroughly, the warning against selfishness. And in what an interesting and pleasing light, his perfect unselfishness presents him to our view!

There is only one other story for this part of our subject; we may call it—

THE TIME TO BE PLEASANT.

"Mother's worried!" said little Maggie, coming into the kitchen with a pout on her lips.

Her aunt Matilda was busy ironing there. She looked at Maggie a moment, and said: "Then this is the very time for you to be pleasant and helpful. Mother was awake, a great deal through the night, with her poor sick baby."

Maggie made no reply. She put on her hat, and walked off into the garden, and kept thinking about what her aunt had just said: "The time to be helpful and pleasant, is when people are worried." "Sure enough," she said to herself, "that's the time when it will do the most good. I remember when I was sick last year, I was so nervous that if any one spoke to me, it almost made me cry; and mother never once got cross or impatient, but was gentle as a lamb. I ought to pay her back now, and I will."

Then she rose from the grass, where she had been sitting, and with a face full of unselfishness, she hastened to the room where her mother sat nursing, and tending a fretful, teething baby. Maggie brought out the pretty ivory balls, and began to jingle them for the little one. He stopped fretting, and a sweet smile passed over his troubled face.

"Couldn't I take him out in his carriage, mother?" she asked. "It is such a fine day."

"I shall be very glad if you will, my dear," said her mother.

The little hat and sack were brought, and baby was soon ready for his ride.

"I'll keep him out as long as I can," said Maggie, "and you must lie down, dear mother, and get a nap while I am gone. You look so very tired."

These kind words, and the kiss which accompanied them, were almost too much for Maggie's mother. The tears rose to her eyes, and her voice trembled, as she said, in reply:

"Thank you, my darling, it will do me a world of good, if you will keep him out an hour or so. The air will do him good too. My head aches badly this morning."

Now just see how much good little Maggie did that day, by trying not to please herself! She was perfectly happy herself. The baby chuckled with delight over his lovely ride; and the poor mother's heart was made to overflow with happiness, at the thought of her dear Maggie's unselfishness. And from all that has now been said, we see how true it is, that when we give way to selfishness it makes us disagreeable; but if we learn the Bible warning against selfishness, it is sure to make us pleasant and agreeable, to those who are about us.

So the second reason why we ought to mind this warning is because selfishness is—a disagreeable thing.

And the third reason why we ought to mind this warning is—because selfishness is a—SINFUL—*thing.*

When we commit sin in most other ways, we only break one of God's commandments at a time. For example, when we disobey our parents, what commandment do we break? The fifth commandment. If we commit murder, which commandment do we break? The sixth. If we steal, what commandment do we break? The eighth. If we bear false witness against our neighbor, what commandment do we break? The ninth. In committing these sins, we only break one commandment at a time. But when we give way to selfishness, *we break six of God's commandments all at once.*

Now you may be ready to ask, can this be possible? Yes, it is. And it is very easy to show how it is.

You know when the ten commandments were first given by God, He wrote them on two tables of stone. On one of these tables, the first four commandments were written. These refer to our duty to God. On the second table, were written the other six commandments. These refer to our duty to our neighbor. When Jesus was on earth, in explaining these commandments, He said that the meaning, or substance of the six commandments, on the second table was, that we should love our neighbors as ourselves. If we have this love in our hearts, it will lead us to keep all the six commandments on the second table of God's Law. But, if we allow selfishness to grow up in our hearts, then it will be impossible for us to love our neighbors as we ought to do. And if we do not love them, we cannot keep the commandments God has given us about our neighbors.

And so it is true, that when we give way to selfishness, we break *six* of God's commandments all at once. And if this is so, then we may well say, that selfishness is—a sinful thing.

THE WARNING AGAINST SELFISHNESS. 375

When we give way to selfishness, we never can tell into what sin it may lead us. We read in the Bible about some of the angels in heaven, who fell into the sin of pride, and who were driven out of that blessed place on account of this sin. But selfishness was the root, out of which that sin grew. And we read of our first parents, who were driven out of the garden of Eden, because they ate of the fruit of the tree, which God had said that they must not eat. But selfishness was at the bottom of their sin. Selfishness is the root out of which *any* sin may grow. It is like carrying powder about us, in a place where sparks are flying all the time. A dreadful explosion may take place at any moment.

Here are some illustrations of the point now before us, that selfishness is a sinful thing. The first may be called

AN OLD MAN'S SELFISHNESS, AND THE SIN TO WHICH IT LED.

A good many years ago there lived in Egypt, an old man, named Amin.

A time of great famine came upon the land, just as it once did in the days of Joseph. Amin had a great store of wheat in his granaries. When bread began to get scarce, his neighbors came to him to buy grain. But he refused to sell it to them. He said he was going to keep his stock till all the rest of the grain in the land was gone, because then he would be able to get a higher price for it. Food became very scarce. People were suffering on every hand. Many died of starvation, and yet this selfish man still kept his stores locked up. At last the hungry people were willing to give him any price he might choose to ask for his grain. Then he smiled a cruel, selfish smile, when he thought how rich his locked up stores of wheat would make him.

He took the iron key of his great granary. He opened the door, and went in. But in a moment, all his hopes of great gain faded away, like a dream. Worms had entered the heaps of his once beautiful grain, and destroyed it all. Hungry as the people were they yet raised a great shout of gladness, for what happened to that wretched man. They saw that it was God's judgment which had come down upon the miserable man, for his selfishness, and that it served him right. But such was the effect of his disappointment upon the old man himself, that he fell down dead at the door of the granary. *His selfishness killed him.* It destroyed his body in this world, and his soul in the world to come.

Here we see how true it is that selfishness is a sinful thing.

Now where is our text to-day? Romans xv. 1. What are the words of the text? "We—ought not to please ourselves." What is the sermon about? The Bible warning against selfishness. How many things about selfishness did we speak of as reasons for minding this warning? Three. We ought to mind this warning, in the first place, because selfishness is what sort of a thing? An *ugly* thing. In the second place, because it is what? A *disagreeable* thing. And in the third place, because it is what? A *sinful* thing.

And in trying to mind this warning against selfishness, nothing will help us so much as to keep the example of Jesus before us. He "pleased not himself." And if we pray that —"the same mind may be in us which was also in Christ Jesus;" and that we may have grace to tread in the blessed steps of His most holy life;" then we shall be able to remember, and carry out the words of our text, "WE OUGHT NOT—TO PLEASE OURSELVES."

INDEX.

A.
	PAGE
A Child's Faith	22-4
An Old Man's Experience	62-3
A Gallon of Whiskey	64
A Child's Answer	68
A heart-broken Wife's Injury	73
A whole Family Destroyed	74-6
A Young Man's sad Story	77-9
A Touching Story	108-11
A Secret Murder found out	150-2
Afraid to Swear Alone	351-2
Anger—The Warning against	162
" —Interferes with our Comfort	163
" —Interferes with our Duty	170-1
" —Interferes with our Safety	179-70
" —The Effect of upon us	183-4
" —How a Boy Minded the Warning against	169-70
Aunt Bessie, the Wonderful	367-8

B.
Bible Warnings are Lighthouses	1
Be in Time	273
Bertie's Industry, or I Can because I Ought	265-6

C.
Content or Discontent	288-9
Contented Tom	300-1

Covetousness—The Warning against 34-5
" —Will destroy our Happiness . . 35-7
" —A man made Unhappy by . . 39-40
" —The terrible Evil of 41-2
" —Will injure our Usefulness . . 43
" —The Evil it did to Judas Iscariot . 44
" —The Evil it did to Ananias and Sapphira 47-8
" —Will lose our Reward . . . 50-4

D.

Dare to say No 89-90
Duty Neglected 107
Diligence Rewarded 269
Discontent—The Warning against 285
" —Mind the Warning against, for our own comfort 286
" —The Fable of the Bittern, about . . 287
" —Mind the Warning against, to please God 302-5
Dr. Todd's Illustration of Disobedience to Parents . 320-1
" " Lectures to Children, Dr. Newton's acknowledgment of indebtedness to . 320

G.

God—We should remember for His sake . . . 1
" —We should remember for Our own sake . 16
" —We should remember, for the sake of Others. 25
Grandfather's Star 26-7
Grieving the Spirit—Warning against . . . 186-7
" " " —Will injure our Knowledge . 188
" " " —Will injure our Happiness . 193-6
" " " —Will injure our Usefulness . 201-2
" " " —The sad Result of . . 209-11
" " " —Will cause the Loss of our Souls 207

INDEX.

H.

How a lazy Boy's Sin found him out.	156-7
" A Swiss Traveller lost his way for want of a Guide	188-9
" Alice found the way to Heaven.	190-2
" To be Beautiful.	296
Honor—Obeying our Parents will bring to us.	310
Hermann Billings, the obedient German Boy.	314-16

I.

"I allus keeps my Word"	124-7
I want to do something for God	13-15
If I had only done my Duty	102-3
It's never too Late to Mend	112
Intemperance—The Warning against,	60-1
" —A costly Sting	61
" —Facts about	67
" —The Pyramid of	72
" —An Injurious Sting	73
" —A Disgraceful Sting	
" —Leads to the loss of the Soul	106
" —A Sailor's Sad Experience of	95-6

J.

Jessie's six Cents	19-22
John Wesley's Contented Spirt.	297
Joseph—The honor obeying his Father, brought to.	310-11

L.

Light-houses, are Warnings	10
Lying—The Warning against	114
" —What God thinks of	115
" —What Men think of	122-3
" —Worse than Stealing	128
" —The Punishment which must follow after Death.	130-1

INDEX.

Lying—Afraid of 132
" —Kept from, by fear of the Future. . . 133-5

M.

Minding God 11
Murderers found out by Birds 157-60
Making up with God 181
Make your own Sunshine 290-1
Moving Mountains 244-7

N.

Not Yet—How these two words brought Ruin. . 17-18
No Treasure in Heaven 55-6
Not letting the Heart down 298-9

O.

One Glass of Rum 65-6
Only once Drunk 86-7
Our Father 349

P.

Playing Drunk 85
Pride—The Warning against 239-40
" —Brings Unhappiness 241
" —Illustrated by a Fable of the Tortoise and
    the Eagle 242-3
" —Brings Trouble 248-50
" —Brings Loss 263 4
Pleasure Found in Obeying our Parents . . . 317
Profit—Results from Obeying our Parents . . 325-7

R.

Rainbow Reagan 28-9
Returning Good for Evil 104-5

S.

Saying Please. 30-2
Selfishness—An Ugly Thing 357-8
" —How a Boy was made Ugly by . . 359-60

INDEX. 383

Selfishness—A Disagreeable Thing	365
" —A Sinful Thing	373
" —Breaks Six Commandments at once	373-4
" —An Old Man's, and the Sin to which it led	375-6
Sabbath Breaking—The Warning against,	214
" " —Mind the Warning against, for our own sakes	214
Sabbath—The, Sir Matthew Hale's opinion about	215-16
" —The, The difference between Honoring and Dishonoring	218-20
Sabbath-Breaking—Mind the Warning against, for the Sake of our Country	221-2
" " —The Effects of	223-4
" " —Mind the Warning against, for the Lord's Sake	229-30
Sabbath—The, Battles on	225
" —The, Keeping Furnaces	226-8
" —The, The Experience of a Working man about	233-5
" —The, A Parable about	236-7
Sin—Sure to be Found out,	138
" —The Presence of God, finds out.	139
" —The Power of God, finds out	145-6
" —How a little Girl's, was found out	148-9
" —The Purpose of God, finds out	153
Slothfulness—For the sake of our Example, we should mind the Warning against	261-1
" —Our Success depends on minding the Warning against	267-8
" —Will cause the Loss of Heaven	274-5
Smile whenever you Can	293
Satisfied with the Best	306-7
Swearing—The Warning against,	334
" —A Disgrace to Ourselves	335
" —What a Little Girl thought of	336
" —The Minister's Reproof of	337-8

Swearing—How a Boston Boy stopped the . . 339
" —An Injury to others 340
" —What a Boy did to stop 341-2
" —In Hebrew 343-4
" —An Offence to God 348
" —How a Little Girl felt about . . . 350
" —Struck Dumb while. 353-4

T.

Tommy Wright Sorely Tempted 303-6
Time Enough Yet 208
The Defective Mill 231-2
Two Kinds of Ladies 251-2
Too Proud to take Advice 253-4
The Printer's Boy 253-4
The Prisoner's Pin 266-7
Three Earnest Christian Ladies . . . 278-80
The Poor Boy and the Preacher . . . 281-2
The Contented Bishop 292
The Fable of the Buckets 296
The Warning against Disobeying our Parents. . 309
The old Doctor's Story 318-20
The Profit of Obedience and Kindness . . 330-2
The Pious Sailor and the Swearing Merchant . 345-7
The time to be Pleasant 371-2

U.

Unselfish—The, Miner Boy 361
" —The, School-Boy 362-4
Usefulness Hindered 104-5

W.

Washington, George—The Honor he gained by
                      obeying his Mother . . 312-13
What a Man lost by not Drinking . . . 69-70
What came to a Boy for minding his Mother . 328-9
Waterloo—Where the Battle of, was gained . 268
Willing to Shovel 270-2

Other Solid Ground Titles

BIBLE PROMISES by Richard Newton
HEROES OF THE EARLY CHURCH by Richard Newton
HEROES OF THE REFORMATION by Richard Newton
THE KING'S HIGHWAY by Richard Newton
THE SAFE COMPASS by Richard Newton
RAYS FROM THE SUN OF RIGHTEOUSNESS by R. Newton
A PATHWAY INTO THE PSALTER *by William Binnie*
THE PSALMS IN HUMAN LIFE *by Rowland E. Prothero*
THE COMMUNICANT'S COMPANION by *Matthew Henry*
THE SECRET OF COMMUNION WITH GOD by *Matthew Henry*
THE MOTHER AT HOME by *John S.C. Abbott*
LECTURES ON THE ACTS OF THE APOSTLES *by John Dick*
THE FORGOTTEN HEROES OF LIBERTY *by J.T. Headley*
LET THE CANNON BLAZE AWAY by *Joseph P. Thompson*
THE STILL HOUR: *Communion with God in Prayer* by *Austin Phelps*
COLLECTED WORKS of James Henley Thornwell (4 vols.)
CALVINISM IN HISTORY *by Nathaniel S. McFetridge*
OPENING SCRIPTURE: *Hermeneutical Manual by Patrick Fairbairn*
THE ASSURANCE OF FAITH *by Louis Berkhof*
THE PASTOR IN THE SICK ROOM *by John D. Wells*
THE BUNYAN OF BROOKLYN: *Life & Sermons of I.S. Spencer*
THE NATIONAL PREACHER: 2nd Great Awakening Sermons
FIRST THINGS: *First Lessons God Taught Mankind* Gardiner Spring
BIBLICAL & THEOLOGICAL STUDIES *by 1912 Faculty of Princeton*
THE POWER OF GOD UNTO SALVATION *by B.B. Warfield*
THE LORD OF GLORY *by B.B. Warfield*
A GENTLEMAN & A SCHOLAR: *Memoir of Boyce by J. Broadus*
SERMONS TO THE NATURAL MAN *by W.G.T. Shedd*
SERMONS TO THE SPIRITUAL MAN *by W.G.T. Shedd*
HOMILETICS AND PASTORAL THEOLOGY *by W.G.T. Shedd*
A PASTOR'S SKETCHES 1 & 2 *by Ichabod S. Spencer*
THE PREACHER AND HIS MODELS *by James Stalker*
IMAGO CHRISTI: *The Example of Jesus Christ by James Stalker*
LECTURES ON THE HISTORY OF PREACHING *by Broadus*
THE SHORTER CATECHISM ILLUSTRATED *by John Whitecross*
THE CHURCH MEMBER'S GUIDE *by John Angell James*
THE SUNDAY SCHOOL TEACHER'S GUIDE *by John A. James*
CHRIST IN SONG: *Hymns of Immanuel by Philip Schaff*
DEVOTIONAL LIFE OF THE S.S. TEACHER *by J.R. Miller*

Call us Toll Free at 1-877-666-9469
Send us an e-mail at sgcb@charter.net
Visit us on line at solid-ground-books.com
Uncovering Buried Treasure to the Glory of God

www.ingramcontent.com/pod-product-compliance
Lightning Source LLC
Chambersburg PA
CBHW021759220426
43662CB00006B/115